MICHEL ROUX
Eggs

MICHEL ROUX
Eggs

PHOTOGRAPHY BY MARTIN BRIGDALE

quadrille

All spoon measures are level unless otherwise stated.

Use fresh herbs, sea salt and freshly ground black pepper unless otherwise suggested.

Egg sizes are given where they are critical, otherwise use medium eggs, preferably organic or free-range. Anyone who is pregnant or in a vulnerable health group should avoid recipes that use raw egg whites or lightly cooked eggs.

Timings are for fan-assisted ovens. If you are using a conventional oven, increase the temperature by 10–15°C (½ Gas mark). Use an oven thermometer to check the temperature.

Editorial director **Anne Furniss**
Creative director **Mary Evans**
Project editor **Janet Illsley**
Translator and editor **Kate Whiteman**
Designer **Lucy Gowans**
Photographer **Martin Brigdale**
Props stylist **Helen Trent**
Production **Rebecca Short** & **Tom Moore**

This edition published in 2018 by Quadrille, an imprint of Hardie Grant Publishing

Quadrille
52-54 Southwark Street
London SE1 1UN
quadrille.com

Cataloguing in Publication Data: a catalogue record for this book is available from the British Library.

Text © Michel Roux 2005
Photography © Martin Brigdale 2005
Design and layout © Quadrille 2018

ISBN 978 1 78713 114 9

Printed in China

Special thanks to my son, Alain Roux, and Chris Lelliott, my senior sous-chef at The Waterside Inn, for their help with the food for photography and recipe testing.

Contents

Introduction

I respect the egg for its genius in all forms of cooking. In my view, it is an undervalued food, invariably overshadowed by expensive, luxury ingredients. So, I have decided that it is time for me to write a book about this most fragile and defenceless of all foods, to bestow the egg with the honour it deserves.

Eggs have been much maligned over the past two decades, variously branded high in cholesterol, difficult to digest, carriers of salmonella and the like. But, in reality, they are highly nutritious – and simple and quick to cook. An egg is a treasure chest of substances that are essential for a balanced diet – rich in proteins, lipids, vitamins and minerals, including iron and zinc. It provides first-class protein, is low in sodium, and a medium egg contains only 78 calories. Ideal for breakfast, lunch, tea, dinner and supper, eggs are also great in sandwiches, an ideal picnic food, and they are essential in the preparation of so many different desserts, cakes and sauces.

Eggs have always fascinated me. I love their oval, sometimes elongated shape, the purity of their lines and the tint of their shells – ranging from natural white to pale nut brown. When I hold an egg in my hand, I feel that it represents the image of the universe, and it awakens and increases my respect for life.

At the age of barely three, I would rush outside whenever I heard Julie, our family hen, cackling to announce that she was about to lay. I would gently collect the still warm new-laid egg and hurry to the kitchen with it. My mother collected the eggs in a large bowl, which would be kept full during the summer; in winter Julie laid only one or two eggs a week – but we loved her just the same.

Like bread, eggs are one of life's most basic and indispensable foods. I first started to discover their professional value when I began my pâtisserie apprenticeship at the age of fourteen. Since then, eggs have become my most faithful kitchen companions and they hold no secrets for me. In this book, I share their secrets with you, offering over 130 recipes and ideas for using eggs. Some are classic, others more modern and creative, but all reflect my personal style.

Different kinds of eggs

Hen's eggs Throughout the world, these are by far the most widely eaten eggs. They are referred to simply as 'eggs', whereas those laid by other birds are specifically named. Hen's eggs vary in weight from 53g (1¾oz) for a small egg to over 73g (2½oz) for a very large one. You can buy lots of different types of hen's eggs; for more information, see page 12.

Bantam eggs Weighing 30–40g (1–1 ½oz), these are of equal quality to hen's eggs. Bantams are small hens, half the size of normal chickens, and their smaller eggs are perfect for babies or dishes where eggs are best featured discreetly.

Duck eggs These weigh 85–95g (3–3½oz) and contain a little more fat than hen's eggs. I am very partial to their rich flavour, which is at its best in soft-boiled and scrambled eggs, omelettes and in desserts.

Goose eggs Weighing 180–200g (6¼–7oz), these have chalky-white, very hard shells and a more pronounced flavour than hen's eggs. Usually I hard-boil and slice them into discs, cover them with a tomato or cheese sauce, and heat in the oven for a few minutes before serving. Sometimes I use them for quiches or my leek flamiche (see page 186).

Pigeon eggs These only weigh about 15g (½oz). They are perfectly pleasant, but nothing special. Indeed I think a pigeon tastes rather better than its egg...

Quail's eggs These attractive little speckled eggs weigh 15–20g (½–¾oz) and they can be cooked in the same way as hen's eggs, though for rather less time. The delicate, creamy texture and fine flavour of quail's eggs makes them very popular, but it is important to avoid overcooking them, even when hard-boiling. They are perfect for canapés and can be eaten in a single mouthful.

Ostrich eggs At the other end of the scale, these weigh 500–600g (18–21oz). The ostrich enabled me to take on the challenge of feeding six people with a single egg, much to the amusement and astonishment of everyone! Ostrich eggs have a pronounced flavour, which needs to be tempered with flavourings like fresh herbs or cheese. They can be used for omelettes and in pâtisserie, but the shells are extremely hard and difficult to crack open.

Gull's eggs These are considered a delicacy in England, where it is only permitted to collect them from around the end of April to mid-May (the exact period varies, according to the weather). I love their flavour and prefer to semi hard-boil them very lightly, so that they remain soft in the middle. I serve them as a starter with celery salt or sweet paprika and buttered wholemeal bread. Gull's eggs are not cheap, but they justify their expense.

There are many other varieties of eggs that are less widely available but perfectly edible. Sometimes obtainable from farmers, poulterers, game dealers and high-class grocers, they include the following:

Guinea fowl eggs Weighing about 30g (1oz), these have a delicate flavour and are ideal as a starter or in a salad.

Pheasant eggs Weighing about 30g (1oz), these have a strong flavour and are best served hard-boiled.

Emu eggs Weighing 350–450g (12oz–1lb) and popular in Australia, these are best scrambled, but can be used in pâtisserie.

Most wild bird's eggs are strictly protected by laws, which prohibit collecting or selling them commercially at any time, or only permit this at specified periods during the year. Contravention of these laws is severely penalised.

Basics

Eggshells are a natural barrier against germs and bacteria, which is ineffective if the shell is cracked or broken. I strongly advise you not to use eggs with damaged shells.

Never break eggs straight into a mixture or into the pan when cooking; first, crack them individually into a ramekin to check that they are fresh.

Eggs must be kept in a cool place, but should always be taken out of the fridge an hour or two before using. Store them in their cartons or in the egg compartment of the fridge with the pointed end downwards to keep the yolk centred in the white.

Egg shells are porous, the yolks readily absorbing both good flavours and undesirable ones, so store eggs apart from any other foods unless you are imparting flavour.

To separate an egg, crack it open over a bowl and gently pass the yolk between the two half shells, allowing the egg white to fall into the bowl. Separated egg whites can be kept for several days in an airtight container in the fridge, or frozen for a few weeks.

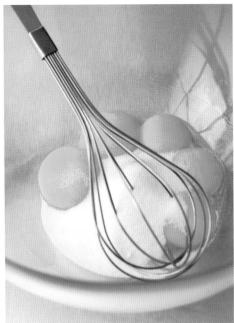

Facts about eggs

Labelling of eggs This varies from country to country. In the UK, the Lion Quality mark indicates that the egg has been produced to higher standards of hygiene and animal welfare than required by EU or UK law. All Lion Quality eggs come from British hens vaccinated against salmonella and carry a 'best before' date, which is 21 days after packing. An additional code on the egg indicates how the hens have been kept: 0 for organic eggs; 1 for free-range eggs; 2 for barn eggs; 3 for eggs produced by caged hens. Special breed hen's eggs are available from many supermarkets, farmer's markets and other specialist suppliers. These often have a denser texture, superior flavour and larger, deeper coloured yolks.

Organic and free-range eggs Organic eggs are widely available. They are produced by hens fed on natural feed (free from additives), which have freedom to roam outdoors and are kept in relatively small flocks. Free-range eggs are produced by hens that also have continuous access to outdoor runs, and a varied diet, though they are usually kept in larger flocks. I advocate the use of organic or free-range eggs, whenever possible.

Egg shell colour This varies according to the breed of chicken. American consumers favour eggs with a white shell, whereas the French and British are more inclined to prefer brown eggs. Some special breed hens produce eggs with pretty coloured shells in a range of pastel shades.

The flavour of an egg This is concentrated in the yolk and is determined by what the chicken eats – corn, wheat etc. Its rich taste is composed of many different elements. Needless to say, you cannot identify these individually when you taste an egg.

Egg sizes Hen's eggs vary in weight from under 53g (1¾oz) for a small egg, 53–62g (1¾–2¼oz) for medium, 63–72g (2¼–2½oz) for large, and over 73g (2½oz) for very large. The only inedible part of an egg is the shell, which weighs about 9g (⅓oz). Of the edible parts of a medium egg, the white weighs about 33g (1¼oz) and the yolk approximately 20g (⅔oz).

Egg whites These are a vital ingredient in soufflés, mousses and meringues, their whisked texture lending extraordinary volume and lightness. Unlike the yolks, egg whites vary significantly according to the size of the egg. I almost always use the whites of medium eggs. If you are unsure, it is best to measure the volume of egg whites: 250ml (1 cup) = 8 medium egg whites; 500ml (2 cups) = 16 whites.

   In many sauces, pastries and other recipes, only the egg yolks are used, and the whites are simply thrown away. This is completely unnecessary, particularly as egg whites freeze extremely well. In fact, they become more glutinous on freezing, which makes them even better for preparing meringues and soufflés.

Freshness If you are in any doubt about the freshness of an egg, do the following simple test: Drop the egg into cold salted water (100g/3½oz salt to 1 litre/4 cups water). If the egg sinks, it is 'extra fresh'; if it remains suspended in the water, it is about 2 weeks old; if it floats, the egg is not fresh enough to be eaten and should be thrown away.

Did you know? A single hen lays around 280 eggs each year. Light, temperature and feed all affect her laying capacity. She needs at least 12 hours of light to conceive an egg and the time between conception and laying is a mere 24–26 hours. And finally, I should mention that a hen has no need of a male mate to produce an egg, which can be produced from a fertilised or unfertilised ovum.

At The Waterside Inn, I use free-range eggs from a local farm. They are supremely fresh, with beautiful deep yellow yolks. I recommend that you buy organic or free-range eggs whenever possible. Those labelled 'extra fresh' guarantee that the eggs have been laid within the past 9 days. 'Fresh' eggs have been laid within 28 days.

A good-quality non-stick frying pan will make all the difference when you are cooking omelettes, fried eggs, crêpes, etc. I use Tefal pans, which give excellent results at both low and high temperatures.

Basics

Use a large balloon whisk or a hand-held electric beater to whisk egg whites and make sure the bowl and whisk are clean and dry. Even a trace of grease, water or egg yolk will prevent the egg whites from reaching their maximum volume. Whisked egg whites should stand in soft peaks – avoid over-whisking.

Very carefully fold whisked egg whites into a mixture, to avoid losing volume by knocking out the air.

The first six chapters of this book showcase eggs as a dish in their own right, covering all the different ways of cooking an egg – boiling, poaching, frying, scrambling, baking and omelettes. The recipes in the subsequent chapters use the amazing culinary properties of eggs to create a variety of dishes, including starters, snacks, main courses, desserts and sauces. Eggs are not necessarily the main ingredient here, but their unique properties are essential to the dish: soufflés, custards, ice creams, meringues, sponges and much more...

Boiled Eggs

Simplicity is the essence of this chapter, for the egg is not only cooked in its shell, but often served in it too. It is essential to use very fresh eggs, especially if they are to be soft-boiled. I have used the same technique for boiling eggs (see page 18) since I was eighteen. It requires neither a watch nor an egg timer and it is infallible – once you've tried it, I am sure you will adopt it forever. Mollet eggs make delectable starters. I love to add them to a rocket (arugula) or dandelion salad, and when I'm in the South of France, I especially enjoy them in tomato nests with crunchy cucumber (see page 28). Hard-boiled eggs have many uses, but they must be cooked carefully to ensure that they don't become rubbery. I always cook them in barely simmering water at around 70°C/150°F to keep the texture supple. They are perfect for a quick snack or a picnic.

Boiled eggs

Take the eggs out of the fridge about 2 hours in advance to prevent them from cracking when the water boils. Or pierce the rounded end of the shell with a pin, to allow air to escape during cooking. Use a pan large enough for all the eggs to lie comfortably. If they knock each other during cooking, the shells may crack and some white will escape.

Soft-boiled eggs Put the eggs in a saucepan, cover generously with cold water and set over a medium heat. As soon as the water comes to the boil, count up to 60 seconds for a medium egg; the egg white will be lightly set.

If you prefer the white slightly firmer but the yolk still runny, cook the egg for another 30 seconds.

For an even firmer white with the yolk just beginning to set, allow 30 seconds more (1½ minutes in total). As soon as the eggs are boiled to your liking, lift them out of the water or they will continue to cook. Serve in egg cups as soon as possible. Take off the tops by tapping the pointed end with a sharp knife.

Mollet eggs Cook as for soft-boiled eggs, but allow only 3 minutes once the water starts simmering. As soon as the water boils, reduce the heat, otherwise if the eggs cook in fast-boiling water the whites will become rubbery. As soon as the eggs are cooked, use a slotted spoon to transfer them to a bowl of very cold water with some ice cubes. Leave to cool for about 10 minutes, then tap the shells with back of a spoon to crack them. To shell the eggs, start at the rounded end where the little air sac is, and peel off the shells under a trickle of cold running water. The water will infiltrate between the solid egg white and the membrane that lines the shell, making it easier to peel the egg without damaging it.

Mollet eggs (soft boiled) Place an egg weighing 55–60g (2oz) into a waterbath or saucepan, with water generously to cover that is set to a constant 62°C/144°F, for 1 hour. The same results can be attained by placing the egg on a baking tray in an oven set at 62°C/ 144°F, for 1 hour. Either chill for later reheating or gently peel by cracking the egg onto the reverse of a slotted spoon, leaving their shape intact. Season and serve either warm or cold, as desired. The egg white will be almost translucent and soft to eat. The egg yolk will be slightly runny and almost 'confit' in taste and texture.

Hard-boiled eggs Boil exactly as for mollet eggs, but cook for 6 minutes after the water starts simmering.

Soft-cooked eggs with pots of flavour

Serve soft-boiled eggs with a selection of delicate flavourings, leaving everyone to mix their preferred ingredients into their egg. Allow two eggs per person – they are bound to be popular, especially if you serve them on a large platter for brunch. Or why not push the boat out and serve them for breakfast in bed with a ramekin of caviar?

Mini-ratatouille Cut a medium onion, a small chunk of red, yellow or green (bell) pepper, a small courgette (zucchini), a dwarf aubergine (eggplant), and a very ripe, skinned tomato into 3–4mm (⅛in) dice. Gently heat 3 tbsp olive oil in a small saucepan, sweat the onion for 2 minutes, then add the pepper and cook for 5 minutes. Add the courgette, then at 2-minute intervals, add the aubergine and tomato. Season with salt and pepper, add a few thyme leaves, and serve just warm.

Olives Choose a few different green and black olives. Stone them, chop larger olives and mix together.

Mini-croûtons Cut the crusts off a slice of white bread and cut the bread into tiny cubes. Heat a little clarified butter (see page 87) in a frying pan and fry the croûtons over a medium heat until golden. Drain well on kitchen paper and serve warm.

Capers The small ones are best. Rinse off the vinegar under cold running water and drain well.

Soft fresh herbs Choose whichever soft herbs you like and snip them finely. My favourites are chervil, flat leaf parsley and chives.

Grated cheese There is nothing better than freshly grated Comté or Parmesan.

Salt and pepper Freshly milled sea salt and cracked pepper are essential.

Boiled eggs with special soldiers

Here is an army of little soldiers to delight the eye and palate. They are all delicious dipped into soft-boiled eggs. Allow one or two soft-boiled eggs per person.

Asparagus tips Peel the stalks with a vegetable peeler, and cook the asparagus for a few minutes in boiling salted water until done to your liking (they are best cooked until firm but not crunchy).

Grissini Wrap grissini bread sticks in thin slices of Parma, Bayonne or Pata Negra ham just before serving.

French fries Cut the potatoes into thin batons and deep-fry until very crisp on the outside but still soft in the middle. Drain on kitchen paper and serve piping hot.

Cheese straws Use ready-made cheese straws, or buy some puff pastry and make your own. Serve warm.

Carrot sticks Peel a few carrots and cut them into very thick, long matchsticks. Blanch in boiling salted water with a pinch of curry powder and a knob of butter added for 30 seconds. Drain well and serve just warm or cold.

Brochettes of Comté cheese To make rosemary skewers, strip the leaves from some fairly woody rosemary stems, leaving a sprig of leaves at the top of each one. Cut the cheese into small cubes and thread 5 or 6 cubes on to each rosemary skewer (from the bare end). If necessary, first make a hole through the cheese cubes with a cocktail stick (toothpick).

Soft-cooked eggs with vanilla caramel & brioche

SERVES 4

4 medium eggs

1 vanilla pod, split lengthways

4 slices of brioche loaf

For the caramel sauce

100 g (½ cup) caster (superfine) sugar

1 tsp lemon juice

For anyone with a sweet tooth, this is breakfast heaven. Be prepared to cook extra eggs as they are addictive! Add a pinch of salt to the caramel for an interesting salty-sweet flavour.

A day in advance, put the raw eggs in an airtight container with the split vanilla pod, and refrigerate for 24 hours. The flavour of the vanilla will permeate the egg shells.

To make the caramel, put the sugar in a heavy-based, deep saucepan and dissolve over a gentle heat, stirring continuously. As soon as it turns to a light caramel colour, turn off the heat and pour in 100 ml (scant ½ cup) boiling water and the lemon juice. Take care as the caramel is liable to splutter and spit. Stir the caramel with a small whisk and cook over medium heat for 2–3 minutes, until it has a syrupy consistency. With the tip of a knife, scrape in a few seeds from the vanilla pod. Pour into a small jug and keep at room temperature.

Toast the brioche slices, remove the crusts and cut into soldiers; keep warm.

Soft-boil the eggs (see page 18) the way you like them, and put them into egg cups. Eat with a teaspoon, letting everyone drizzle some caramel over their egg and dip their brioche soldiers into the soft yolks.

Mollet eggs with rocket & Parmesan shavings

SERVES 4

400g (14oz) rocket (arugula) leaves

6 tbsp Swiss vinaigrette (see page 280)

4 medium eggs

100g (3½oz) Parmesan, shaved into curls

If you are using wild rocket, which has a more peppery flavour than the cultivated variety, you may prefer to add a little oak leaf lettuce to soften the flavour.

Wash the rocket in cold water, drain and keep cool. Dress the rocket with the vinaigrette and divide between 4 plates.

Cook the mollet eggs (see page 18) and peel them. Cut the eggs in half lengthways and arrange on the rocket salad. Scatter on the Parmesan shavings and serve.

Mollet egg & courgette tarts with spinach sabayon

200 g (7oz) flan pastry (see page 180), or use ready-made shortcrust

flour, to dust

150 g (5½oz) courgettes (zucchini), cut into thick sticks

3½ tbsp olive oil

1 garlic clove, unpeeled and halved

1 thyme sprig

4 medium eggs

1 tsp snipped basil leaves

salt and freshly ground pepper

1 quantity spinach & watercress sabayon (see page 276)

To make the pastry cases, roll out the pastry on a lightly floured surface to a 3 mm (⅛in) thickness and cut out four 10 cm (4in) rounds, with a pastry cutter. Use these to line 4 tartlet tins, about 7 cm (2¾in) diameter (see page 182). Refrigerate for 30 minutes. Meanwhile, preheat the oven to 200°C/400°F/Gas 6.

Prick the base of each pastry case several times with a fork, line with a disc of baking paper and fill with baking beans or dried beans. Bake blind for 10 minutes, then remove the beans and paper, lower the oven setting to 180°C/350°F/Gas 4, and bake for a further 5 minutes. Unmould and keep at room temperature.

Put the courgettes in a small saucepan with the olive oil, garlic and thyme, and cook very gently for 4–5 minutes. Remove the garlic and thyme, and leave the courgettes in the oil at room temperature.

Cook the mollet eggs (see page 18) but don't peel them.

Drain the courgettes thoroughly, then mix with the basil and seasoning to taste. Divide between the pastry cases. Put the mollet eggs in a bowl, cover with boiling water for 30 seconds, then drain and peel. Place a mollet egg in each pastry case. Arrange on warm plates, coat generously with the sabayon and serve, as a starter.

illustrated on page 276

Mollet eggs in tomato nests with crunchy cucumber

SERVES 4

4 beef or Marmande tomatoes, about 200g (7½oz) each

salt

1 cucumber, about 400g (14oz)

4 medium eggs

400ml (1¾ cups) bagnarotte sauce (see page 269)

4 chervil sprigs

For the marinade

150ml (scant ⅔ cup) white wine vinegar

75g (6 tbsp) caster (superfine) sugar

few rosemary needles

pinch of salt and freshly ground pepper

All the ingredients for this easy starter can be prepared in advance and assembled at the last moment. The refreshing crunchy cucumber adds a touch of sweetness and acidity, which contrasts well with the tomato.

First make the marinade. Put all the ingredients in a saucepan with 40ml (2½ tbsp) water, bring to the boil, then strain through a chinois into a bowl. Keep at room temperature.

To skin the tomatoes, make a slit in the top and cut out the cores. Plunge the tomatoes into boiling water for 10–15 seconds until the skins start to split, refresh in iced water, then peel off the skins. Cut a sliver off the bottom of each tomato so that they stand upright. Slice off the tops and scoop out the flesh and seeds with a spoon. Season the insides with salt, invert on to kitchen paper and leave to drain.

Using a vegetable peeler, peel the cucumber along its length on one side only. Cut a bit off both ends. Using a mandolin, shave the skin side of the cucumber into 2mm (1/16in) thick ribbons and place in the marinade. Deseed the other half of the cucumber and finely dice the flesh. Add to the marinade with the ribbons, leave for 3 minutes, then drain.

Cook the mollet eggs (see page 18) and peel them. Mix a little bagnarotte sauce into the diced cucumber and divide between the tomatoes. Put a cucumber ribbon into each tomato, leaving the border overhanging the top. Put a mollet egg into each nest, coat lavishly with bagnarotte sauce, top with a sprig of chervil and serve.

Mollet bantam eggs on crabmeat & celeriac julienne

SERVES 4

1 celeriac, about 450g (1lb)

1 quantity Swiss vinaigrette (see page 296) 280

250g (9oz) fresh white crabmeat

juice of ½ lemon

salt and freshly ground pepper

4 bantam eggs

1 tender lettuce heart, about 8 leaves

½ lemon, cut into 4 wedges

2 tbsp flat parsley leaves

You can use frozen or canned crabmeat for this starter, but fresh crab has a superior flavour. If you cannot find bantam eggs, use ordinary hen's eggs.

Peel the celeriac with a sharp knife, discarding all the hard bits, and cut into julienne on a mandolin. Toss with 4 tbsp of the Swiss vinaigrette and keep at room temperature.

Check the crabmeat carefully, removing any cartilage and fragments of shell. Mix the crabmeat with the lemon juice and season with salt and pepper to taste.

Cook the mollet eggs (see page 18), allowing 1½ minutes only for bantam eggs, then peel them.

Divide the celeriac between 4 plates. Pile the crabmeat in a dome in the centre and top with the bantam eggs. Arrange a couple of lettuce leaves, a lemon wedge and some parsley on one side. Drizzle a little vinaigrette over the eggs and serve the rest separately. Serve chilled.

Hard-boiled egg & smoked eel ciabatta sandwich

Serves 4

1 ciabatta loaf, about 28 x 10 cm (11¼ x 4in)

150g (5½oz) mayonnaise (see page 266), or use ready-made

50g (1¾oz) pesto (see page 197), or use ready-made

100g (7 tbsp) butter, softened

salt and freshly ground pepper

For the filling

50g (1¾oz) baby spinach, shredded

100g (3½oz) smoked eel, thinly sliced

100g (3½oz) tomatoes, thinly sliced

1 avocado, stoned, peeled and thinly sliced

4 hard-boiled eggs (see page 18)

50g (1¾oz) snipped chives

100g (3½oz) cucumber, peeled and thinly sliced

1 tbsp basil leaves

150g (5½oz) mozzarella, thinly sliced

50g (1¾oz) Cheddar or Gruyère, grated

I truly adore this regal and scrumptious sandwich with its medley of hot and cold filling ingredients. My wife, Robyn, makes it as a surprise treat on my days off, or on holiday. You can vary the ingredients – substitute raw or cooked ham or hot bacon for the eel, for example.

Put the ciabatta on a board and slice it lengthways, with a serrated knife, two-thirds above the base to make a sort of long lid. Using the knife and scraping with a fork, remove a little of the soft crumb from the lid and two-thirds from the base. Mix the mayonnaise with the pesto and set aside.

Preheat the grill. Spread the softened butter all over the inside of the ciabatta and season lightly with salt and pepper. Grill the base and lid until almost golden. Layer all the filling ingredients into the base, in the order listed opposite, placing the eggs lengthways and pressing each layer lightly with your fingertips. Spread half the mayonnaise/pesto mixture over the spinach layer, and the rest over the basil leaves. Finish with a layer of mozzarella slices, topped with the grated cheese.

Place the filled ciabatta base under the grill (broiler) for 5–6 minutes. Reheat the cut side of the lid for 2 minutes. Replace the lid on the ciabatta base, pressing down lightly with your fingertips. Use a palette knife to slide the ciabatta on to a board and present it whole at the table before cutting it into thick slices with a serrated knife to serve.

Mini Scotch eggs

SERVES 4

8 quail's eggs

300g (10½oz) pork fillet or shoulder, trimmed and finely minced

1 egg white

2 tsp snipped parsley and chives

salt and freshly ground pepper

small pinch of cayenne

2 medium eggs

2 tbsp milk

seasoned flour, to dust

100g (1¼ cups) fine white breadcrumbs, to coat

300ml (1¼ cups) groundnut oil, to deep-fry

These are best eaten slightly warm as a starter, or you can serve them cold for a picnic or as canapés. A garnish of raw or deep-fried celery leaves is perfect. Serve mayonnaise or a spicy relish on the side.

Hard-boil the quail's eggs (see page 18), allowing 2½–3 minutes after the water starts simmering. Peel and pat dry with kitchen paper.

In a bowl, mix the pork with the egg white, parsley, chives, salt, pepper and cayenne. Take about an eighth of this mixture and lightly flatten it in the palm of your hand. Place a boiled quail's egg in the middle and gently mould the meat around the egg; it should not be more than 4mm (⅛in) thick. Repeat with the other quail's eggs.

Beat the eggs with the milk and season with salt and pepper. Roll the Scotch eggs in the seasoned flour, taking care not to spoil the shape, and dust off any excess. Dip each one into the egg mixture, then roll in breadcrumbs to coat evenly.

Heat the oil for deep-frying in a deep pan to 180°C/350°F. Deep-fry the Scotch eggs, a few at a time, for 1½–2 minutes. Lift out with a slotted spoon and drain on kitchen paper.

Hard-boiled eggs stuffed with mussels

SERVES 4

32 mussels, scrubbed

50ml (3½ tbsp) dry white wine

4 hard-boiled eggs (see page 18)

150g (¾ cup) mayonnaise (see page 266)

2 tbsp lemon juice

salt and freshly ground pepper

3 tbsp groundnut oil

200g (7oz) carrots, peeled and cut into fine julienne

½ red onion, finely chopped

Put the mussels and wine in a saucepan, cover with a tight-fitting lid and cook for a few minutes until the shells have steamed opened. Lift out the mussels, shell them and place in a bowl, discarding any that have not opened. Strain the cooking juices through a muslin-lined sieve into the bowl with the mussels. Keep at room temperature.

Cut the hard-boiled eggs in half lengthways and carefully remove the yolks. Press the yolks through a coarse strainer to make egg mimosa.

Drain the mussels thoroughly, straining the juices into a saucepan. Reduce over a low heat to a syrupy consistency. Cool, then stir into the mayonnaise. Mix in the mussels and arrange 3 or 4 mussels in each egg white cavity.

Put the lemon juice in a bowl with some salt and pepper, then whisk in the oil. Mix in the carrot julienne and chopped onion. Spoon on to a platter, arrange the stuffed eggs on top, and sprinkle with egg mimosa. Serve cold, but not chilled.

Alternative fillings

Grilled squid finely diced and mixed with my bagnarotte sauce (see page 269), served with a garnish of salmon eggs.

Brown shrimps mixed with finely diced boiled potatoes, flavoured with Caesar dressing (see page 279) and generously sprinkled with snipped chives.

Herb salad with hard-boiled eggs & tuna brochettes

SERVES 4

2 goose eggs (or 4 duck or hen's eggs)

1 tsp yellow mustard seeds

For the tuna brochettes

2 green (bell) peppers

560g (1lb 4oz) fresh tuna fillet

3 tbsp olive oil

For the herb salad

2 tbsp white wine vinegar

salt and freshly ground pepper

6 tbsp groundnut oil

40g (1½oz) flat parsley leaves

20g (¾oz) chervil sprigs

20 chives, cut into short lengths

1 shallot, finely chopped

I've used goose eggs for his modern version of a salade niçoise, but duck eggs or ordinary hen's eggs work equally well.

Hard-boil the eggs (see page 18), allowing 12 minutes for goose eggs after the water starts simmering. Peel and cut into quarters.

For the brochettes, peel the green peppers with a potato peeler, cut into quarters and remove the white membrane and seeds. Cut the flesh into 3cm (1¼in) squares, blanch in boiling water for 1 minute, then drain. Cut the tuna into 12 cubes and brush lightly with olive oil. Thread the peppers and tuna alternately on to 4 skewers, starting and finishing with a pepper square.

For the herb salad, mix the wine vinegar, a little salt and pepper and the groundnut oil in a bowl, then delicately mix in the herbs and shallot.

Heat a griddle pan until very hot. Add the brochettes and sear on one side for 45 seconds or so, to mark a lattice marking. Repeat on every side, cooking for a total of 3–4 minutes for tuna that is still pink in the middle.

Divide the salad between 4 plates and arrange a tuna brochette on top. Place the hard-boiled egg quarters alongside and sprinkle with mustard seeds to serve.

Poached Eggs

From breakfast to lunch and through to supper, poached eggs are a real treat. Serve them plain or with a sauce, on toast, floating in a soup, or sitting atop my onion tartlets (see page 57). It is easy to poach eggs neatly draped in their whites, and it takes only 5 minutes of your time. A word of advice – don't add salt to the water as it hinders the white compacting and studs it with tiny holes. In 1982, my brother Albert and I accepted the challenge to cook a dinner for 3,500 people at the Royal Albert Hall. The first course was a classic Roux Brothers' dish oeuf poché Albert, comprising artichoke bases, smoked salmon mousse and poached eggs, topped with a slice of smoked salmon. It took a brigade of four chefs led by my nephew, Michel Roux Junior, a day and a half to poach 3,500 eggs to perfection – truly the stuff of nightmares!

Poached eggs

Poached eggs are usually eaten as soon as they are ready, but they can be cooked ahead and kept in cold water in the fridge for up to 2 days. To reheat, immerse the poached eggs in a bowl of boiling water for 30 seconds only.

Half-fill a wide saucepan, about 10 cm (4in) deep, with unsalted water. Add 3 tbsp white wine vinegar and bring to the boil.

Break an egg into a ramekin or small bowl and tip it gently into the pan, at the point where the water is bubbling.

Repeat with the other eggs, but do not poach more than 4 eggs at a time. Poach for about 1½ minutes.

Using a slotted spoon or small skimmer, lift out the first egg and press the outside edge lightly to check if it is properly cooked.

As soon as the egg is cooked to your liking, remove it with the skimmer or slotted spoon. Either serve immediately, or transfer to a bowl of iced water and leave for about 10 minutes.

Trim the edges with a small knife to make a neat shape. This will also cut off the excess white that inevitably spreads during cooking.

The poached egg is now ready.

Eggs Benedict

SERVES 4

2 English muffins

100g (7 tbsp) butter

100g (3½oz) spinach, washed and stalks removed

salt and freshly ground pepper

4 small slices of cured tongue

4 poached eggs (see page 42)

200ml (scant 1 cup) hollandaise sauce (see page 262)

few chives, snipped into short lengths

I learnt this classic recipe many years ago at the British embassy in Paris. Ham is often substituted for tongue, but I don't think it does justice to this simple yet grandiose dish, which is best eaten for brunch or as a starter.

Split the muffins and toast them lightly for a minute or two. Keep them warm.

Heat half the butter in a frying pan and cook the spinach for 1–2 minutes until just wilted. Season with salt and pepper and keep warm. Heat the rest of the butter in the same pan and warm the tongue slices for 1–2 minutes.

Immerse the poached eggs in boiling water for no more than 30 seconds to warm through, then drain thoroughly.

Put half a muffin on each plate and top with a slice of tongue, some spinach and a hot poached egg. Coat generously with hollandaise sauce, sprinkle with chives and serve immediately, with the rest of the hollandaise sauce served separately.

Eggs florentine

SERVES 4

60g (¼ cup) butter

600g (1lb 5oz) spinach, washed
and stalks removed

2 pinches of sugar

salt and freshly ground pepper

50ml (3½ tbsp) double (heavy)
cream

freshly grated nutmeg

50g (1¾oz) Comté (if possible),
or Parmesan, freshly grated

250g (1 cup) hot Mornay sauce
(see page 282)

4 poached eggs (see page 42)

There are three elements to success here – the quality of the
spinach, a good Mornay sauce, preferably with Comté cheese,
and perfectly poached eggs. For a tempting variation, replace
the cheese with mushrooms.

In a frying pan over a high heat, melt half the butter. As soon as it
has melted, add half the spinach and sprinkle with a pinch each of
sugar and salt. Give the spinach a stir and cook for 1 minute until
just wilted, then tip into a colander and drain well. Repeat with the
rest of the butter and spinach. Put the drained spinach in a saucepan,
add the cream, season with a pinch of nutmeg, salt and pepper, and
keep warm.

When ready to serve, divide the spinach between 4 egg dishes
or crème brûlée dishes and place in a low oven to keep warm.
Preheat the grill (broiler). Mix half of the grated cheese into the
Mornay sauce. Put the poached eggs in a bowl and cover them with
boiling water for 30 seconds. Drain well and place on top of the
spinach in the dishes.

Coat the hot poached eggs generously with the sauce, then scatter
over the rest of the cheese and pop under a hot grill until it turns
light nut-brown. Serve piping hot.

Poached eggs with prawns & confit tomatoes

SERVES 4

300g (10½oz) cooked prawns or shrimps in the shell

½ tsp curry powder

200g (scant 1 cup) mayonnaise (see page 266)

salt and freshly ground pepper

1 quantity confit tomatoes (see page 134)

1 avocado

juice of 1 lemon

4 poached eggs (see page 42)

All the elements of this starter can be prepared a day ahead and simply arranged on the plates at the last moment.

Peel all the prawns, leaving eight with their heads still attached for the garnish; set these aside. Dissolve the curry powder in 1 tbsp warm water, then add to the mayonnaise, mixing thoroughly with a whisk. Delicately mix in the prawns and season with salt and pepper to taste.

Cut the confit tomatoes into 1cm (½in) wide strips. Peel the avocado with a sharp knife and cut into quarters, discarding the stone. Thinly slice each quarter, keeping it intact at one end, then fan out and sprinkle with a few drops of lemon juice.

To serve, divide the prawns in mayonnaise between 4 plates, top each serving with a poached egg, and arrange an avocado fan on top. Scatter the confit tomato strips around the prawns and garnish the edge of the plates with the whole prawns.

Poached eggs on potatoes with smoked haddock

SERVES 4

300g (10½oz) piece smoked haddock fillet

350g (12oz) small new potatoes, preferably purple, washed

salt and freshly ground pepper

600ml (generous 2½ cups) milk

1 small bouquet garni

40g (2½ tbsp) butter, plus extra to grease

80g (2¾oz) shallots, finely chopped

4 poached eggs (see page 42)

300ml (1¼ cups) sauce écossaise (see page 281)

Serve this dish accompanied with a watercress or rocket salad for a light lunch.

Soak the smoked haddock in cold water for 30 minutes.

Put the potatoes in a pan, cover with cold water and add salt. Boil gently for 20 minutes or until tender when pierced with a knife tip. Pour a little cold water into the pan to stop the cooking process and let cool. When cold, peel and slice the potatoes.

Drain the fish, place in a pan and pour on the milk to cover, adding a little cold water if needed. Add the bouquet garni. Slowly bring to a simmer and poach gently for 5 minutes. Leave the haddock to cool in the milk until almost cold.

Heat the oven to 160°C/315°F/Gas 2½. Melt the butter in a small pan, add the shallots and sweat gently for 2 minutes. Grease 4 individual gratin or egg dishes generously with butter. Mix the shallots with the sliced potatoes and divide between the dishes, then flake the haddock over the top. Cover with foil and heat in the oven for 5 minutes.

Meanwhile, reheat the poached eggs in boiling water for no more than 30 seconds. Drain thoroughly and put a poached egg on top of the potatoes in each dish. Coat with piping hot sauce écossaise and serve.

Herby poached eggs in mousseline potato nests

SERVES 4

300g (10½oz) potatoes, preferably Desirée or King Edward

salt

about 150ml (scant ⅔ cup) milk

40g (2½ tbsp) butter

4 poached eggs (see page 42)

2 tbsp snipped soft herbs (parsley, chervil, chives)

roast chicken or pork pan juices, skimmed

Peel the potatoes, cut into pieces and place in a pan. Cover with cold water, add a pinch of salt, and cook at a gentle boil for about 20 minutes until tender when pierced with a knife tip. Drain the potatoes and rub through a mouli or sieve into a saucepan.

Bring the milk to the boil. Place the potatoes over a low heat and, with a wooden spoon, mix in the butter, then the boiling milk. Season to taste with salt.

Warm the poached eggs in boiling water for 30 seconds, drain well and roll them in the snipped herbs.

Divide the potato between 4 deep plates and make a well in the centre with the back of a spoon. Put a poached egg in each well and pour the warm chicken or pork juices round the eggs and all round the potatoes. Serve immediately.

illustrated on previous page

Caesar salad with poached eggs

SERVES 4

12 canned white anchovy fillets

a little milk, to soak (optional)

2 Cos lettuces, trimmed

2 slices of white bread

60g (¼ cup) clarified butter (see page 87) or groundnut oil

½ quantity Caesar dressing (see page 279)

100g (3½oz) Parmesan, in one piece

4 poached eggs (see page 42)

2 tbsp chopped curly parsley

This delicious salad, with the addition of a poached egg, makes the perfect light lunch, dinner or snack. To enjoy it at its best, serve the salad very cold, but not chilled.

If necessary, soak the anchovy fillets in cold milk for 30 minutes to remove excess salt.

Discard the greenest outer leaves from the lettuces. Cut the rest into 4cm (1½in) chunks, wash in cold water and drain thoroughly. Keep in the fridge.

To make the croûtons, remove the crusts from the bread, then cut into 1cm (½in) cubes. Heat the clarified butter or oil in a frying pan and fry the bread cubes, turning, until golden all over. Drain in a colander, then on kitchen paper.

Put the lettuce into a large bowl, pour the dressing over and mix delicately but thoroughly. Pile the lettuce into 4 deep plates. Scatter on the croûtons and arrange 3 anchovy fillets on each salad. Finely shave the Parmesan over the salad, using a vegetable peeler.

Roll the poached eggs in the chopped parsley and place one in the middle of each salad. Serve immediately.

illustrated on page 278

Poached egg in a light vegetable soup

1kg (2lb 2oz) very ripe tomatoes

1 lettuce, about 400g (14oz)

60g (¼ cup) butter

1.25 litres (5 cups) chicken stock or water

150g (5½oz) potatoes, peeled and diced

salt and freshly ground pepper

6–8 poached eggs (see page 42)

This healthy, nourishing soup is quick to make and always popular with guests. Make sure you use ripe, flavourful tomatoes.

Skin, quarter and deseed the tomatoes. Dice some of the tomato flesh or cut into diamonds; you need a spoonful for each serving; set aside. Trim the lettuce and wash it in cold water. Finely shred 2 or 3 leaves and keep with the reserved tomato. Shred the rest of the lettuce.

To make the soup, melt the butter in a pan, add the shredded lettuce and sweat over a medium heat for 3 or 4 minutes. Add the tomatoes, stock or water, and the potatoes. Bring to the boil, then cook over medium heat for 8–10 minutes, until the potatoes are tender.

Blitz the soup in several batches in a blender for 2 minutes, then pass it through a chinois into a clean saucepan. Season with salt and pepper to taste.

Warm the poached eggs in boiling water for a few seconds, then drain. Put one in the middle of each warm soup bowl and pour the soup around the eggs. Scatter the reserved lettuce and tomato over the surface and serve at once.

Poached eggs on onion tartlets

SERVES 4

2 large onions, about 500g
(1lb 2oz) total weight

100g (7 tbsp) butter

150ml (scant ⅔ cup) double
(heavy) cream

few thyme leaves, plus sprigs
to garnish

salt and freshly cracked pepper

350g (12oz) ready-made puff
pastry, or flan pastry (see
page 180)

flour, to dust

4 small hen's or bantam eggs,
poached (see page 42)

I sometimes add a little fresh goat's cheese to the cream and onions, which makes them even more delicious.

Cut the onions into thin slices. Melt the butter in a heavy-based saucepan over a low heat. Add the onions and cook gently for 45 minutes, stirring every 10 minutes. Pour in the cream, add the thyme leaves and simmer for another 20 minutes or so. Season with salt and pepper and tip into a bowl; set aside.

To bake the tartlets, preheat the oven to 170°C/325°F/Gas 3. Roll out the pastry on a lightly floured surface to a 3mm (⅛in) thickness. Using a 12cm (4½in) plain round pastry cutter, cut out 4 discs and place on a baking sheet. Rest in the fridge for about 20 minutes.

Prick each pastry disc 4 or 5 times with a fork. Spread the onions evenly on top of the discs, then bake for 25–30 minutes; the bottom of the pastry should be well cooked and crisp.

Put the poached eggs in a bowl, carefully pour on boiling water and leave them for 30 seconds only to warm through. Drain well and put a poached egg on each onion tartlet. Top with a sprig of thyme and serve on warm plates.

Fried Eggs

To fry eggs to perfection, all that is needed is to brush the pan with a thin film of melted or softened butter. I cannot abide fried eggs swimming in butter or oil; they aren't at all healthy and I find them totally indigestible. Follow my healthier technique for classic fried eggs (see page 60) unless you prefer a crunchy fried egg, in which case I suggest you try my method for deep-frying eggs (see page 74). 'Oeufs sur le plat' are another variation on the fried egg theme. For these, the eggs are cooked in buttered heatproof dishes over indirect heat (see page 68). For me, the perfect partner for fried eggs is ham or bacon, as in the classic ham & eggs (see page 63). The very thought of fried eggs on steak burgers (see page 67) makes my mouth water, and as for 'oeufs sur le plat' with morels (see page 73), they are irresistible.

Fried eggs

Eggs for frying should always be very fresh. Use a good-quality non-stick frying pan for cooking.

Heat a non-stick frying pan until just warm, then brush with softened butter. When the butter is hot, add the eggs one at a time. It is best to break the egg into a ramekin or small bowl first, then slide it into the pan.

If you like your eggs as well cooked on the top as on the bottom, cover the pan for 30 seconds or up to 1 minute. I prefer this method to turning them over with a palette knife, as there is less risk of piercing or breaking the yolks.

When the eggs are done as you like them, take them out of the pan with a palette knife. Season with salt and pepper just before serving.

Ham & eggs

30g (2 tbsp) butter

2 small slices of cooked ham,
cut off the bone if possible

2 eggs

salt and freshly ground pepper

The secret of good ham and eggs is top quality ham and
a very gentle heat. This classic dish is so often ruined by
overcooking the ham.

In a non-stick frying pan, melt the butter over a low heat. Put in
the ham and turn the slices over after 1 minute, just long enough
to warm them through.

Break an egg into a ramekin and slide it gently on to a slice of ham,
then repeat with the other egg. Cook gently until the fried eggs are
done as you like them (see page 60).

Slide a palette knife under each slice of ham and place the ham and
eggs on plates. Season lightly with salt and pepper.

Fried quail's eggs on toast with mustard hollandaise

Serves 6

2 slices of white bread

60g (¼ cup) softened butter

1 tsp white wine vinegar

2 tbsp groundnut oil

salt and freshly ground pepper

60g (2oz) mâche (corn salad), trimmed and washed

6 quail's eggs

100g (scant ½ cup) mustard hollandaise (see page 265)

Cut out 6 rounds from the bread with a 4cm (1½in) pastry cutter. Toast under the grill (broiler), then brush on one side with half of the softened butter; keep warm.

Mix the wine vinegar and oil with a little salt and pepper, and toss the mâche in this dressing.

Brush a warm non-stick frying pan with the rest of the softened butter, heat the pan and fry the quail's eggs (see page 60), allowing 1½–2 minutes. Remove from the pan and trim to neaten, using a 4cm (1½in) plain pastry cutter.

Put a toast round on each warm plate, buttered side-up, and place a fried quail's egg on top. Partially coat the eggs with the mustard hollandaise and put another spoonful of sauce on one side of the plate. Arrange the mâche on the other side. Serve immediately, as a starter.

Fried eggs on steak burgers

SERVES 4

600g (1lb 5oz) beef steak (preferably rump or sirloin), trimmed of all sinews and fat

salt and freshly ground pepper

60ml (¼ cup) groundnut oil or clarified butter (see page 87)

4 medium eggs

softened butter, to fry

I serve this dish with French fries or mousseline potatoes and green beans or a green salad. To fully appreciate the flavour of the meat, it's best not to serve condiments or a sauce – but that's up to you...

Mince the beef through the fine grill of a mincer or, better still, chop it with a knife as finely as possible. Season with salt and pepper. Place an 8cm (3¼in) plain pastry cutter on a piece of cling film (plastic wrap) and put one-quarter of the meat in the middle. Flatten it with the back of a spoon, then carefully lift off the cutter. Repeat to make another 3 steak burgers.

Heat the oil or clarified butter in a frying pan or griddle pan. Put in the burgers and fry over a high heat for 1–2 minutes on each side to seal them, then reduce the heat and cook until done to your liking. A rare burger will take 3–4 minutes; cook for another 2–3 minutes for medium.

At the same time, fry the eggs in a buttered non-stick frying pan until cooked to your liking (see page 60). Trim to neat rounds, using a 5cm (2in) plain pastry cutter.

Using a palette knife, carefully place a fried egg on each steak burger. Transfer to plates and serve at once.

Oeufs sur le plat

Lightly brush the inside of a heatproof egg dish with softened butter.

Place the dish over indirect heat (using a heat diffuser) and put in 1 or 2 eggs, depending on the size of the dish. I recommend breaking the eggs into a ramekin or small bowl first, then sliding them into the dish.

Cook the eggs for 3–4 minutes until done as you like them. If you like, place under a hot grill (broiler) for 20 seconds to cook the yolks a touch more. Serve in the dish.

'Oeufs sur le plat' with parsley beurre blanc

SERVES 4

8 eggs

60g (¼ cup) softened butter, to grease dishes

For the parsley beurre blanc

30g (1oz) shallots, chopped

150ml (scant ⅔ cup) dry white wine

1 tbsp double (heavy) cream

60g (¼ cup) butter, diced

2 tbsp snipped flat parsley leaves

salt and freshly ground pepper

This delectable butter sauce is the ideal complement to oeufs sur le plat. Its slight acidity counteracts the richness of the egg yolks and enhances the flavour.

First make the beurre blanc. Put the chopped shallots in a small pan and add the white wine. Bring to the boil and reduce over a medium heat by two-thirds. Add the cream and let bubble for a few moments. Whisk in the diced butter, then take the pan off the heat and add the snipped parsley. Season with salt and pepper; keep warm.

Brush 4 egg dishes with softened butter. Break 2 eggs, one at a time, into a ramekin, and slide them into one dish. Repeat with the other 6 eggs. Cook the eggs to your liking (see left).

Spoon the parsley beurre blanc over the eggs and serve immediately.

'Oeufs sur le plat' with sorrel & tomato coulis

SERVES 2

12 small, tender sorrel leaves

30g (2 tbsp) softened butter

4 eggs

for the tomato coulis

1 large, very ripe tomato, skinned, deseeded and diced

2½ tbsp olive oil

1 small garlic clove, chopped

1 thyme sprig

salt and freshly ground pepper

This dish is a delight. The sorrel adds a touch of acidity, contrasting with the mellowness of the egg, and the natural freshness of the tomato gives it a lift.

First make the tomato coulis. Put the tomato, olive oil, garlic and thyme in a small pan and cook over a low heat for about 10 seconds, until the tomato is softened. Immediately discard the thyme and blitz the tomato in a blender for a few seconds. Season with salt and pepper; keep warm.

Cut two of the sorrel leaves into fine julienne and keep for the garnish.

Brush the base of 2 egg dishes with the softened butter. Arrange the rest of the sorrel in the egg dishes and set them on a heat diffuser over a medium heat until the sorrel begins to wilt. Immediately break 2 eggs into a ramekin and slide them on to the sorrel in one dish. Repeat with the other 2 eggs. Cook until done to your liking (see page 68).

Serve the eggs in their dishes. Scatter over the sorrel julienne and pour the tomato coulis around the edge. Serve at once.

'Oeufs sur le plat' with asparagus tips & coulis

Serves 4

24 small asparagus spears

salt and freshly ground pepper

40g (2½ tbsp) butter, plus 60g (¼ cup) softened butter to grease dishes

1 shallot, finely chopped

8 eggs

1 tbsp snipped flat parsley leaves

Asparagus is the perfect partner for an egg.

Thinly peel the lower part of the asparagus stalks. Cut off the tips leaving 3cm (1¼in) stalk attached. Dice the lower part of the stalks. Cook the asparagus tips in boiling salted water for 1–2 minutes, depending on whether you like them crunchy or just firm. Refresh in cold water and drain.

To make the coulis, melt the 40g (2½ tbsp) butter in a small pan. Add the shallot and diced asparagus stalks, cover and sweat very gently for 3 minutes. Add 100ml (scant ½ cup) water and cook, uncovered, over a medium heat for 5 minutes. Purée in a blender, then pass through a chinois into a small pan. If the coulis is not thick enough, reduce it over a low heat for a few minutes, until it lightly coats the back of a spoon. Season to taste and keep hot.

Brush 4 egg dishes with butter. Arrange 6 asparagus tips at the edge of each dish. Break 2 eggs, one at a time, into a ramekin, then slide into an egg dish. Repeat with the other dishes. Cook to your liking (see page 68).

Put a dish on each plate and pour a little coulis over the asparagus tips. Sprinkle with the parsley, and serve the rest of the coulis separately.

'Oeufs sur le plat' with morels

Serves 4

400g (14oz) fresh morels, or 100g (3½oz) dried

60g (¼ cup) butter, plus 60g (¼ cup) softened butter to grease dishes

1 shallot, finely chopped

2 tbsp double (heavy) cream

salt and freshly ground pepper

8 eggs

1 tbsp snipped chervil leaves

The flavour of this dish is absolutely divine when it is made with fresh morels in season. It's the perfect starter for a special lunch.

Pare the fresh morels with a small sharp knife, cut off the bottom of the stalks, and halve larger morels lengthways. Rinse in cold water to eliminate all traces of sand or grit, and drain well. If you are using dried mushrooms, put them in a large bowl and cover with plenty of boiling water. Leave for 2 hours, then drain.

Heat 60g (¼ cup) butter in a frying pan set over a medium heat and add the morels. Fresh morels will cook in 4–6 minutes; allow 3–4 for dried. Add the shallot and cook gently for 1 minute. Stir in the cream and cook for a further 30 seconds. Season with salt and pepper to taste. Keep warm.

Lightly brush the inside of 4 egg dishes with softened butter. Break 2 eggs, one at a time, into a ramekin, and slide them into a dish. Repeat with the other 6 eggs. Cook to your liking (see page 68).

Put 2 fried eggs on each plate. Divide the morels between the plates, arranging them around the eggs. Sprinkle the snipped chervil over the eggs and serve immediately.

Crunchy fried eggs

Two-thirds fill a small, heavy-based saucepan with groundnut oil and heat over a medium heat to 180°C/350°F.

Break an egg into a ramekin or small bowl and gently slide it into the hot oil. After a few seconds, the egg will begin to fry. Use two wooden spatulas or spoons to lift any egg white that has spread out back over the egg to maintain a rounded shape.

After 1 minute, carefully turn the egg over in the oil so that it cooks evenly.

After 1½–2 minutes, the egg will be crunchy on the outside and the yolk will still be slightly runny. Lift it out of the oil with a slotted spoon and drain on kitchen paper.

The sooner you serve the egg, the better it will be. It is best to fry the eggs individually, but you can cook two at a time if you do it very carefully.

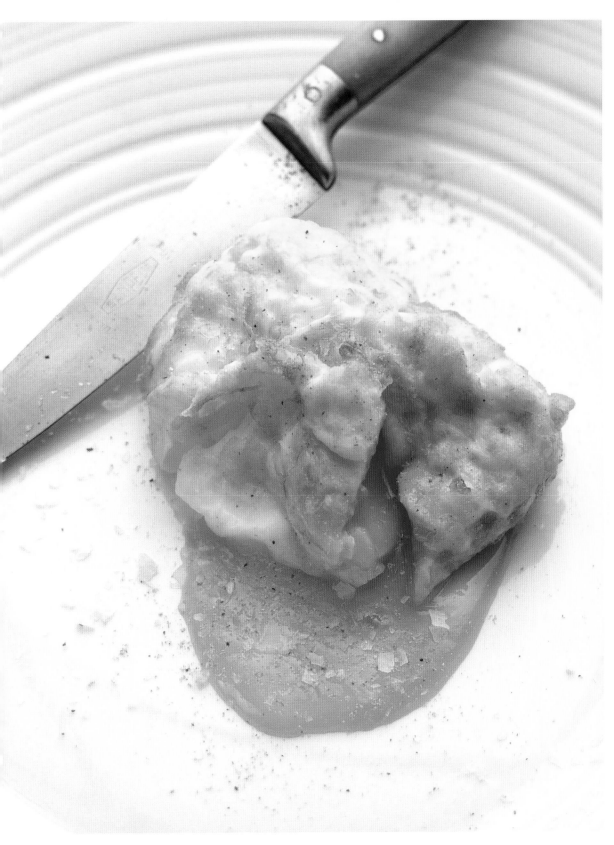

Crunchy fried eggs in a nest of grilled aubergines

SERVES 4

2 long aubergines (eggplants), about 250g (9oz) each

50ml (3½ tbsp) olive oil

salt

groundnut oil, to deep-fry

4 large eggs

20g (⅔oz) curly parsley leaves, washed and well dried

With a very sharp knife, cut the aubergines lengthways into 4–5mm (¼in) thick slices, discarding the outer slices. Place the aubergine slices in a dish, brush with the olive oil and salt lightly.

Heat a griddle pan until very hot. Add 3 or 4 aubergine slices and cook for 1 minute, then give them a quarter-turn and cook for another minute to mark a grid lattice pattern. Turn the slices over and repeat on the other side. Put them in a dish lined with greaseproof paper and keep warm.

Heat the groundnut oil in a heavy-based, deep saucepan and deep-fry the eggs to your liking (see page 74). Drain on kitchen paper.

Lower the temperature of the oil slightly to 160°C/350°F, drop in the parsley, stir with a slotted spoon and deep-fry for 1 minute until very crisp. Remove with the spoon and drain on kitchen paper.

Arrange the aubergine slices like little nests on 4 plates. Put a fried egg in each cavity and scatter with fried parsley. Serve immediately.

Crunchy fried eggs on Darphin potatoes with spinach

SERVES 4

Serve a pear chutney or salsa on the side of this, if you like.

250g (9oz) potatoes, Desirée or King Edward

salt and freshly ground pepper

3 tbsp groundnut oil, plus extra to deep-fry

1 tbsp red wine vinegar

80g (⅓ cup) clarified butter (see page 87), or 80ml (⅓ cup) groundnut oil

4 eggs

40g (1½oz) tender baby spinach leaves, washed and drained

Peel the potatoes, then cut into fine julienne on a mandolin. Place in a salad bowl, without rinsing so that the starch is retained. Salt lightly and leave for 3–4 minutes.

Combine the 3 tbsp groundnut oil, the wine vinegar and a little salt and pepper to make a vinaigrette.

To make the Darphin potatoes, use 4 small frying pans, about 10 cm (4in) in diameter if you have them; otherwise, use one large pan. Heat the clarified butter or oil in the pan(s). Squeeze the potatoes in a cloth to dry. Put them into the pan(s) and flatten into uniform cake(s), pressing them with a palette knife. Cook over a medium heat for 3–4 minutes, until golden brown, then turn them over with the palette knife and cook the other side for 3–4 minutes. Drain on kitchen paper.

Heat the groundnut oil for deep-frying in a suitable pan and cook the eggs to your liking (see page 74). Drain on kitchen paper.

Delicately mix the spinach leaves into the vinaigrette. If you've made a single, large Darphin, cut into portions with scissors. Put a potato cake on each plate and top with a fried egg. Arrange the dressed spinach around the eggs and the potatoes.

Crunchy fried eggs
on dandelion salad

Serves 4

400g (14oz) very tender yellow or
green dandelion leaves, trimmed

6 tbsp groundnut oil, plus extra
to deep-fry

2 tbsp white wine vinegar

salt and freshly ground pepper

1 large white onion, peeled

100ml (scant ½ cup) milk

50g (6 tbsp) plain (all-purpose)
flour, to dust

pinch of paprika

4 eggs

30g (1oz) shallots, finely chopped

I adore this. The crisp fried eggs and onion marry perfectly
with the dandelion leaves, and transform a classic rustic
dandelion salad into something very special.

Wash the dandelion leaves in very cold water, drain well and place
in the fridge. Make a dressing with 6 tbsp oil, the wine vinegar and
salt and pepper to taste.

Cut the onion into thin rings and soak in the milk for 5 minutes,
then drain. Season the flour with a pinch of salt and a smidgeon
of paprika. Sprinkle the onion rings very lightly with the seasoned
flour. Heat 200ml (scant 1 cup) groundnut oil in a deep frying pan
to 180°C/350°F. Drop in the onion rings and fry until just golden and
crisp. Drain and reserve on kitchen paper.

Heat the groundnut oil for deep-frying in a heavy-based, deep
saucepan and cook the eggs to your liking (see page 74). Drain
on kitchen paper.

Mix the dandelion leaves with the dressing and chopped shallots.
Divide between 4 plates and place a fried egg in the middle. Scatter
some onion rings around and serve at once.

Scrambled Eggs

Scrambling is the finest way to cook eggs in my opinion. My brother, Albert, uses the classic method of cooking them slowly in a bain-marie, but I prefer the quicker, more modern approach of scrambling eggs in a pan over a low heat on a heat diffuser. Perfect for breakfast, lunch or a weekend brunch, they always look inviting, whether you present them on a plate, on toast or in warm pitta bread. For a taste of Mexico, I mix them with snipped herbs, chopped tomatoes and diced red onions, and serve them cold in tacos. When truffles are in season, simply macerate a few raw truffle peelings or trimmings in the eggs for several hours, then scramble them to make the most perfect dish imaginable. The recipes in this chapter take account of the seasons and they are some of my favourite egg dishes. I encourage you to try them all...

Scrambled eggs

SERVES 2

Allow 2 medium eggs per person for a starter or light snack, or 3 medium eggs per person for a main course.

Melt 40 g (2½ tbsp) butter in a shallow, heavy-based pan set on a heat diffuser over a low heat, or in a bain-marie. Break 4–6 eggs into a bowl and beat very lightly with a fork. Tip into the pan with the hot, melted butter and stir.

Cook over a low heat, stirring gently and more or less continuously with a wooden spoon.

It will take 3–4 minutes for the eggs to become just set, but very creamy. (If using a bain-marie, allow about 6 minutes). If you prefer firmer, dryer scrambled eggs, cook for another 2 minutes.

When the eggs are scrambled to your liking, add 2 tbsp cream or a knob of butter, and season with salt and pepper. Scrambled eggs are best served immediately.

Scrambled eggs 'magda' on fried bread

SERVES 2

3 slices of white bread, 5mm (¼in) thick

80g (⅓ cup) clarified butter (see below)

40g (2½ tbsp) butter

4 eggs, beaten

1 tbsp cream

salt and freshly ground pepper

1 tbsp strong Dijon mustard

1 tbsp snipped flat parsley leaves, plus extra leaves to garnish

1 tbsp snipped chives

30g (1 oz) Gruyère, grated

Clarified butter
This will withstand a higher frying temperature than butter. It is also used for making emulsified sauces, such as Hollandaise (see page 262). To make about 80g (⅓ cup) clarified butter, heat 100g (7 tbsp) unsalted butter in a pan over a low heat and slowly bring to the boil. Skim off the froth from the surface, then carefully pour the clarified butter into a bowl, leaving the milky sediment behind. Clarified butter will keep in the fridge for several weeks.

Cut off the crusts from the bread, then cut the slices diagonally in half. Heat the clarified butter in a frying pan over a medium heat until hot, then fry the bread triangles until golden on both sides. Keep warm on kitchen paper.

Melt the butter in a heavy-based saucepan, add the beaten eggs and scramble (see page 84). Add the cream at the end of cooking and season with salt and pepper. Stir in the mustard, snipped herbs and grated Gruyère, and adjust the seasoning.

Put 3 fried bread triangles on each plate, overlapping them slightly. Spoon the scrambled eggs on top, garnish with parsley leaves and serve immediately. An ideal winter breakfast.

Scrambled eggs in small potatoes with salmon eggs

SERVES 8

32 small new potatoes, (about 400g/14oz), preferably Charlotte, washed

salt and freshly ground pepper

80g (⅓ cup) butter

8 eggs, beaten

2 tbsp cream

30g (1oz) sevruga caviar

30g (1oz) lumpfish roe

60g (2oz) salmon eggs

If you're feeling extravagant, top the potatoes with real caviar only.

Put the potatoes in a saucepan, cover with lightly salted cold water and cook for about 15 minutes. To check if they are cooked, slide in a knife tip; it should meet with no resistance. Turn off the heat and pour a little cold water into the pan to stop the cooking. Leave the potatoes to cool completely, then drain and pat dry.

Cut off a 5mm (¼in) thick lid with a sharp knife, then using a melon baller or coffee spoon, scoop out the insides of the potatoes, leaving a 5mm (¼in) layer in the skins. Season lightly with salt and pepper, cover with cling film (plastic wrap), and set aside.

Melt the butter in a heavy-based saucepan, add the beaten eggs and scramble (see page 84). Add the cream at the end of cooking and season with salt and pepper. Tip the scrambled eggs into a bowl and set over a bowl of cold water with ice cubes added. Keep stirring the eggs every 2 or 3 minutes until the eggs are cold, then remove the bowl from the iced water.

Fill the potatoes generously with scrambled egg and top each one with a little caviar, lumpfish roe or salmon eggs. Arrange the potatoes on a platter to serve as canapés, or allow 4 per person for a starter.

Scrambled eggs in smoked salmon papillotes

SERVES 4

4 good slices of smoked salmon, about 120g (4¼oz) each

15g (½oz) dill

80g (⅓ cup) butter

8 eggs, beaten

4 tbsp cream

salt and freshly ground pepper

1 lemon, cut into quarters

Serve these papillotes with a lemony cucumber salad for a perfect brunch or lunch.

Trim the smoked salmon to make neat rectangles or squares; set aside at room temperature. Finely dice the trimmings and put them in a bowl. Reserve 4 dill sprigs for the garnish, snip the rest and add to the diced salmon.

Melt the butter in a heavy-based saucepan, add the beaten eggs and scramble (see page 84). Add the cream at the end, then the diced salmon and snipped dill. Season with salt and pepper.

Lay the smoked salmon slices on a sheet of cling film (plastic wrap). Put the scrambled eggs in the middle of the slices and fold one side of the salmon over the eggs, then the other to make papillotes. Turn them over.

Using a palette knife, lift each papillote on to a plate. With a very sharp knife, make a 5cm (2in) long incision in the top to reveal some of the egg. Arrange a dill sprig in each slit, put a lemon quarter on each plate and serve at once.

Scrambled eggs with crab & asparagus tips

SERVES 4

36 small asparagus spears

salt and freshly ground pepper

80g (⅓ cup) butter

8 eggs, beaten

2 tbsp cream

8 cooked shelled crab claws, or 160g (5¾oz) cooked white crabmeat

5g (⅛oz) chives, cut into short lengths

For optimum flavour, use the meat from a freshly cooked live crab. My clients love this dish; it was a great favourite of my friend Egon Ronay.

Peel the asparagus stalks thinly with a vegetable peeler and cut off the tips leaving about 4cm (1½in) stalk attached to them. Cook in boiling salted water for 2–3 minutes; the asparagus should be firm but not crunchy. Refresh in cold water and keep at room temperature.

Melt the butter in a heavy-based saucepan, add the beaten eggs and scramble (see page 84). Add the cream at the end of cooking and season with salt and pepper.

Steam the crabmeat or shelled claws for 2–3 minutes to heat them, then add the asparagus and steam for another minute, until just hot.

Divide the scrambled eggs between 4 plates. Place 2 crab claws or a pile of crabmeat in the centre, arrange the asparagus tips around the crab, scatter with the chives, and serve at once.

Scrambled eggs clamart

SERVES 4

12 small mangetout (snow peas)

100g (3½oz) shelled fresh peas or frozen petits pois

½ lettuce, or 6–8 outer lettuce leaves

100g (7 tbsp) butter

8 eggs, beaten

2 tbsp cream

salt and freshly ground pepper

The vegetables add a touch of sweetness to this delicate, fresh dish, which makes a lovely starter in spring or early summer, when the first fresh peas and mangetout appear in the market. Use an outdoor-grown lettuce if possible.

Slice the mangetout on the diagonal, then cook briefly in boiling water; they should still be crunchy. Drain, refresh in cold water and set aside. Cook the peas briefly in boiling water until barely tender; drain, refresh and set aside.

Wash the lettuce leaves in cold water, drain well and snip them finely into shreds. Place in a saucepan with 20g (1½ tbsp) butter and sweat gently for 1–2 minutes; keep warm.

Melt the remaining butter in a heavy-based saucepan, add the beaten eggs and scramble (see page 84). Add the cream at the end of cooking and season with salt and pepper.

Heat the peas and mangetout in boiling water for 20 seconds, then drain. Mix the peas and lettuce into the scrambled eggs. Divide between 4 plates and arrange the mangetout in the middle. Serve at once.

Scrambled eggs with rhubarb

SERVES 4

200g (7oz) very tender young rhubarb

100g (½ cup) sugar

2 slices of white bread, 1cm (½in) thick

100g (7 tbsp) clarified butter (see page 87)

80g (⅓ cup) butter

8 eggs, beaten

4 tbsp cream

salt and freshly ground pepper

This dish, which I created a good twenty years ago, still makes an occasional appearance on the Waterside Inn menu. The acidity of the rhubarb contrasts perfectly with the egg.

Peel the rhubarb if it is slightly stringy, wash in cold water and drain. Finely dice two-thirds of the rhubarb and cut the rest into small batons or large matchsticks.

Dissolve the sugar in 100ml (scant ½ cup) water in a pan over a low heat, then bring to the boil. Add the diced rhubarb and cook for 30 seconds, then remove with a slotted spoon and place in a bowl; keep warm. Bring the syrup back to the boil, add the rhubarb batons and cook for 45 seconds–1 minute, until just firm. Drain and set aside.

Cut off the crusts from the bread and cut the slices into large cubes. Heat the clarified butter in a frying pan and fry the bread cubes over a medium heat until golden all over. Drain on kitchen paper.

Melt the butter in a heavy-based saucepan, add the beaten eggs and scramble (see page 84). Add the cream at the end of cooking, then the diced rhubarb. Season with salt and pepper.

Divide the scrambled eggs between 4 plates and scatter over the rhubarb batons and the croûtons. Serve immediately.

Portuguese-style scrambled eggs

SERVES 4

4 small clusters of cherry tomatoes (5–6 on each stalk)

50ml (3½ tbsp) olive oil

1 garlic clove, crushed

salt and freshly ground pepper

80g (⅓ cup) butter

8 eggs, beaten

2 tbsp cream

pan juices from roast chicken, lamb or pork, skimmed of fat

12 flat parsley leaves, to garnish

Pan juices from a roast add a wonderful complexity to the eggs in this rich dish, which is nonetheless refreshing, thanks to the tomatoes. It is perfect for a light lunch.

Soak the clusters of cherry tomatoes in cold water for 20 minutes. Preheat the oven to 100°C / 200°F/Gas ¼. Mix the olive oil with the garlic. Drain the tomato clusters and brush them generously with garlicky oil. Sprinkle with a little salt, place on a rack set over a roasting pan and cook in the oven for 20 minutes.

Melt the butter in a heavy-based saucepan, add the beaten eggs and scramble (see page 84). Add the cream at the end of cooking and season with salt and pepper.

Divide the scrambled eggs between 4 deep plates. Put a cluster of cherry tomatoes in the middle of each portion and pour a ribbon of warm chicken or meat juices around the eggs. Garnish with parsley leaves and serve immediately.

Scrambled eggs masala

SERVES 2

4 eggs

2 tbsp milk

1 tbsp finely chopped coriander (cilantro)

salt

30g (2 tbsp) butter

2 tbsp groundnut oil

1 red onion, about 150g (5½oz), finely chopped

1 small green chilli

pinch of ground red pimento

150g (5½oz) tomatoes, skinned, deseeded and diced

warm croissants or flaky parathas

My friend Rasoi Vineet Bhatia cooks these scrambled eggs exquisitely. I love to serve them while on holiday in Provence, under the summer skies. They bring India to my door and introduce a feeling of serenity.

Break the eggs into a bowl, whisk in the milk and chopped coriander, and season lightly with salt.

Heat the butter and oil preferably in a wok, or a non-stick frying pan. Add the onion and sweat gently until it turns pink. Meanwhile, halve and deseed the chilli, remove the white membrane, then finely dice the flesh. Add to the onion with the pimento and tomatoes, and cook for 3–4 minutes.

Pour the beaten eggs into the wok or pan, stirring with a spoon, and scramble lightly for about 1 minute, until soft and creamy.

Serve the scrambled eggs on warm plates, accompanied with warm croissants or flaky parathas.

Baked Eggs

Baked eggs 'en cocotte' are deliciously delicate. They can be prepared in advance and kept in their ramekins in the fridge, ready to cook in a bain-marie just a few minutes before serving. I adore all the recipes in this chapter, but my favourite is truffled eggs en cocotte (see page 105). Nicole, the wife of my dear pâtissier friend, Frédéric Jouvaud from Carpentras, always makes this dish for me when I visit them during the truffle season. Naturally, the truffles come from nearby Mont Ventoux. To impart flavour, Nicole puts a few truffles in an airtight box with the eggs a day before my arrival. When she breaks the eggs into the ramekins, they release the most wonderful truffle aroma. It is agonising waiting while the eggs are baking in the oven! I particularly love to prepare this recipe for a celebration, such as New Year's Eve dinner.

Baked eggs

Bring the eggs to room temperature. Preheat the oven to 170°C/325°F.

Brush the insides of the ramekins or cocottes with softened butter, stopping 1cm (½in) below the rim. Season the dish lightly with salt and pepper.

Carefully break an egg into a small dish and tip it gently into the ramekin. Repeat with the rest.

Drizzle a little double (heavy) cream (about 1 tbsp) on to each egg white, taking care that none runs on to the yolk.

Line a shallow roasting pan with greaseproof paper. Put in the ramekins and gently pour boiling water around them to come halfway up the moulds. Place in the oven.

Check the baked eggs after 10 minutes; the egg white should be just set but the yolk should still be runny. If you prefer your egg a little more cooked, bake for another 2–3 minutes.

Truffled eggs en cocotte

SERVES 4

4 eggs

60g (2oz) fresh black truffles

6 tbsp double (heavy) cream

30g (2 tbsp) softened butter

salt and freshly ground pepper

60g (2oz) Emmenthal or Comté, grated

This is a great favourite at The Waterside Inn, where it features on the menu when fresh truffles are in season – from December to February.

Put the eggs in an airtight container with the truffles and keep in the fridge for at least 24 hours, or 48 hours if possible to allow the aroma of the truffles to permeate the eggs.

Slice the truffles as thinly as possible. Bring the cream to the boil in a small saucepan, then immediately drop in the truffles and turn off the heat. Stir the truffles into the cream with a spoon, cover the pan, and set aside until almost cold.

Preheat the oven to 170°C / 325°F/Gas 3. Brush the insides of 4 cocottes or ramekins, about 8cm (3¼in) in diameter and 4 cm (1½in) deep, with the softened butter and season with salt and pepper. Put three-quarters of the grated cheese into one cocotte and rotate it to coat the inside. Tip the excess cheese into a second cocotte and repeat to coat all 4 dishes.

Divide the cooled cream and truffle mixture between the cocottes. Carefully tip an egg into each one, sprinkle on the remaining cheese, and bake the eggs (see page 102) until cooked to your liking.

Put a cocotte on each plate and serve.

Baked eggs with chicken livers & shallots in wine

SERVES 4

200ml (scant 1 cup) red wine, preferably Pinot noir

1 thyme sprig

1 bay leaf

1 shallot, finely sliced

50ml (3½ tbsp) veal stock, or 100ml (scant ½ cup) chicken stock

2 chicken livers, trimmed of sinews

1 tbsp groundnut oil

salt and freshly ground pepper

30g (2 tbsp) softened butter

4 eggs

Serve these cocottes with small slices of toasted country bread

Preheat the oven to 170°C / 325°F/Gas 3. Put the wine, thyme and bay leaf in a small saucepan and reduce by half over a low heat. Add the shallot and veal or chicken stock, and reduce until thick enough to generously coat the back of a spoon. Discard the thyme and bay leaf and set aside the shallot in wine.

Cut the chicken livers into small pieces. Heat the oil in a small frying pan and quickly sear the livers for 30 seconds. Season, put into a bowl and set aside.

Brush the insides of 4 cocottes or ramekins, about 8cm (3¼in) in diameter and 4cm (1½in) deep, with the softened butter and season lightly with salt and pepper. Mix the chicken livers with the wine and shallots, season to taste, and divide between the cocottes. Carefully tip an egg into each one and bake the eggs (see page 102) until cooked to your liking.

Put a cocotte on each plate and serve immediately.

Baked eggs with smoked ham
& toasted hazelnuts

SERVES 4

30g (2 tbsp) softened butter

salt and freshly ground pepper

4 eggs

80g (2¾oz) lightly smoked ham, diced

4 tbsp double (heavy) cream

8 freshly toasted skinned hazelnuts, halved

Smoked ham and eggs are in perfect harmony here, and the toasted nuts add a contrasting texture and flavour. Serve with toast.

Preheat the oven to 170°C / 325°F/Gas 3. Take 4 cocotte moulds, preferably glass, about 6cm (2½in) in diameter and 6cm (2½in) deep, and brush with softened butter. Season lightly with salt and pepper.

Carefully tip an egg into each mould, then scatter the diced ham and spoon the cream over the egg whites. Bake the eggs (see page 102) until cooked to your liking.

Put a cocotte on each plate. Arrange 4 toasted hazelnut halves around each egg yolk and serve immediately.

Illustrated on previous page

Baked eggs with smoked haddock & grain mustard

SERVES 4

120g (4¼oz) lightly smoked haddock

300ml (1¼ cups) milk

6 tbsp double (heavy) cream

1 tbsp Meaux or grain mustard

salt and freshly ground pepper

30g (2 tbsp) softened butter

4 eggs

1 tbsp snipped flat parsley leaves

Put the haddock and milk in a small saucepan, bring to the boil over a low heat, and then immediately take the pan off the heat. Leave the haddock to cool slowly in the milk; it will finish cooking as it does so.

Preheat the oven to 170°C / 325°F/Gas 3. Drain the smoked haddock, remove the skin and flake the flesh. Heat the cream in a small pan. As soon as it comes to the boil, add the flaked haddock and take the pan off the heat. Stir in the mustard and season to taste. Keep at room temperature.

Brush the insides of 4 cocottes or ramekins, about 8cm (3¼in) in diameter and 4cm (1½in) deep, with softened butter, then season lightly with salt and pepper. Divide the haddock and cream mixture between the cocottes. Carefully tip an egg into each one and bake (see page 102) until cooked to your liking.

Put a cocotte on each plate, sprinkle with snipped parsley and serve immediately.

Baked eggs with brown shrimps & capers

Serves 4

48 cooked brown shrimps or
28 prawns in the shell

30 g (2 tbsp) softened butter

salt and freshly ground pepper

4 eggs

4 tbsp double (heavy) cream

24 small capers, rinsed and well
drained

It's impossible to resist these little shrimps, which are divine with the eggs and cream, and perhaps a slice of toast on the side. One egg is enough for a starter, but I would serve two for a lunch or light main course.

Preheat the oven to 170°C / 325°F/Gas 3. Peel the shrimps or prawns, leaving eight with their heads attached for the garnish.

Take 4 cocotte moulds about 8 cm (3¼in) in diameter and 4 cm (1½in) deep, and brush with the softened butter. Season lightly with salt and pepper. Carefully tip an egg into each mould, drizzle the cream over the egg whites, then scatter the peeled shrimps and capers over the yolks. Bake the eggs (see page 102) until cooked to your liking.

Serve immediately, garnished with the whole shrimps or prawns.

Eggs en cocotte with girolles

SERVES 4

125g (4½oz) girolles

20g (1½ tbsp) softened butter, plus 30g (2 tbsp) for the cocottes

200ml (scant 1 cup) double (heavy) cream

juice of ½ lemon

2 tsp snipped flat parsley leaves

leaves from 1 small thyme sprig

salt and freshly ground pepper

4 eggs

hot toast fingers

If girolles are not available, use ceps, black trumpets or button mushrooms instead. This dish is perfect as a starter, but if you want to serve it as a main course, allow 2 eggs per person.

Preheat the oven to 170°C / 325°F/Gas 3. Clean the girolles, scraping off any earth or sand with a small knife, then wipe gently with a slightly damp cloth. Cut 4 thin slices from the middle of the best girolles and reserve. Finely chop the rest.

Heat the 20g (1½ tbsp) butter in a small frying pan and sauté the mushroom slices for 30 seconds on each side until golden; set aside for the garnish.

Pour two-thirds of the cream into a pan and boil over a medium heat until reduced by one-quarter. Add the chopped girolles and lemon juice, and cook gently for about 5 minutes. Take off the heat, add the parsley and thyme, season to taste and leave to cool.

Brush the insides of 4 cocottes or ramekins, about 8cm (3¼in) in diameter and 4cm (1½in) deep with softened butter and season lightly. Divide the cream and girolle mixture between the dishes. Carefully tip an egg into each one and pour the rest of the cream over the whites. Bake the eggs (see page 102) until cooked to your liking.

Place a cocotte on each plate and put a sautéed girolle slice on top of each egg. Serve immediately with fingers of hot toast for dipping into the yolks.

French toast 'eiderdown' with herbs & bacon

SERVES 8

8 streaky bacon rashers, derinded

40g (2½ tbsp) softened butter

8–10 medium-thick slices of good-quality white bread

3 tbsp snipped chives

3 tbsp snipped flat parsley leaves

3 tbsp snipped chervil

1 tbsp snipped tarragon

4 spring onions (scallions), finely snipped

75g (2½oz) Emmenthal, grated

75g (2½oz) Cheddar, grated

30g (1oz) Parmesan, grated, plus 3 tbsp to finish

salt and freshly ground pepper

8 eggs

800ml (3½ cups) milk

Fry the bacon briefly in a dry frying pan until golden brown, no more than 1½ minutes. Cut into 5cm (½in) pieces and set aside on a plate.

Brush a rectangular or oval ovenproof baking dish, about 26 x 18 x 6cm (10½ x 7 x 2½in), generously with the softened butter. Remove the crusts from the bread and cut each slice into 3 wide strips. Mix together the herbs and spring onions. Combine the grated cheeses.

Cover the bottom of the dish with a layer of bread, season with salt and pepper, and scatter over some of the herb mixture. Sprinkle with a layer of grated cheese, and finally a sprinkling of bacon. Repeat these layers, then finish with a layer of bread; it should be about 1cm (½in) below the rim of the dish.

Beat the eggs with the milk and seasoning. Pour over the bread, sprinkle with Parmesan and cover with cling film (plastic wrap). Leave in the fridge for 24 hours or, better still, 48 hours.

To cook, preheat the oven to 170°C / 325°F/Gas 3. Bake the dish for about 45 minutes, until the mixture has risen 3–4cm (1½in) above the rim and is beautifully golden. Check the cooking by inserting a knife tip into the centre; it should come out clean. Serve from the oven, while still soft in the middle. A great favourite with children.

Little Parmesan & fontina flans

2 eggs

100ml (scant ½ cup) single (light) cream

200ml (scant 1 cup) double (heavy) cream

100g (3½oz) fontina, grated

30g (1oz) Parmesan, grated

pinch of freshly grated nutmeg

salt and freshly ground pepper

20g (1½ tbsp) softened butter

For a brunch or summer buffet, bake one flan in a large gratin dish, allowing an extra 15 minutes in the oven; serve with a salad.

Break the eggs into a large bowl, beat them with a fork as for an omelette, then add both the creams and beat until smooth. Mix in the cheeses and season with nutmeg, very little salt and as much pepper as you wish.

Preheat the oven to 160°C / 315°F/Gas 2½. Brush the insides of 6 cocottes or ramekins, about 8cm (3¼in) in diameter and 4cm (1½in) deep, with softened butter and season lightly with salt and pepper. Divide the egg mixture between the cocottes.

Stand the dishes in a shallow ovenproof dish lined with greaseproof paper. Pour in just enough boiling water to come halfway up the sides of the cocottes, then place in the oven. Check the cooking after 15–20 minutes; the little flans should be just set at the edge and slightly trembling in the middle. Take the cocottes out of the bain-marie and leave on a wire rack to cool.

Serve the flans in the cocottes on plates. They are best served cold, but not chilled.

Omelettes

Omelettes are quick to prepare, simple to cook, easy to digest, and perfect for a one-dish meal. The great food writer Elizabeth David often spoke about her passion for omelettes when she ate at Le Gavroche. Her book *An Omelette and a Glass of Wine* is testimony to her love of omelettes and I was flattered to be asked to write a foreword. Depending on taste, an omelette can be well cooked, moist, or runny in the middle (baveuse), which is how I like it. In my view, the colour should be very light golden; some prefer a deeper shade and others like their omelettes very pale, which I call anaemic. You can also make an omelette using only egg whites. My favourite definition of the perfect omelette (from Mlle Cécile de Rothschild) is well rounded, with just a touch of colour; delicate to touch, squidgy and soft 'as a baby's bottom'.

Omelettes

Allow 2 eggs per person for a starter or light snack; allow 3 eggs per person for a main course.

Break the eggs into a bowl, season with salt and pepper and beat lightly with a fork. Heat a 20 cm (8in) frying pan, preferably non-stick. When the pan is hot, quickly brush a little clarified butter (see page 87) over the inside. Pour in the beaten eggs and cook for 5–10 seconds, until they are just beginning to set very lightly on the bottom.

Immediately scrape the sides towards the middle, using the side of a fork. Carry on stirring almost continuously, gently shaking the pan with your other hand, until the omelette is cooked to your taste.

Allow 1 minute for a lightly cooked 'runny' omelette; 1½ minutes for a firm omelette, or 2 minutes if you prefer a well cooked omelette.

To roll the omelette, flip one half over towards the middle, while tilting the pan. Add the filling, if you are using one (see suggestions overleaf), then roll the omelette over itself completely. Roll the omelette on to a plate or serving platter. Using a knife tip, make an incision down the whole length to expose a little of the filling, then brush with a little clarified butter.

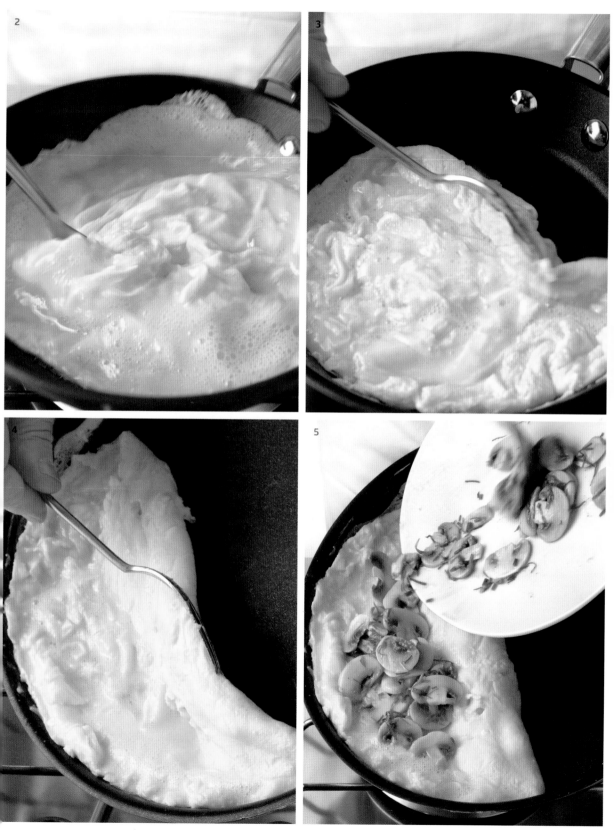

Suggested omelette fillings

I adore filled omelettes; here are some of my favourite fillings, all serve two.

Mushroom omelette Slice 100 g (3½oz) button mushrooms and sauté in butter for 2–3 minutes with a little snipped flat leaf parsley or chives. When wild mushrooms are in season, use girolles or ceps instead of button mushrooms.

Cheese omelette The classic cheese omelette is filled with grated Gruyère. However, I prefer to use fresh goat's cheese. Lightly soften 60 g (2oz) fresh goat's cheese in a bain-marie, then mix with some halved and stoned black olives and spread over the half-rolled omelette before rolling it completely.

Lyonnaise omelette Cut 150 g (5½oz) peeled potatoes into small cubes and sauté in butter for 5 minutes. Add 150 g (5½oz) very thinly sliced onions and cook for another 6–8 minutes. Season with salt and pepper to taste and fill the omelette before rolling it.

Tomato and basil omelette Skin and deseed 250 g (9oz) tomatoes, chop into small pieces and cook gently in 3 tbsp olive oil for 20 minutes. Season the cooked tomatoes with salt and pepper, add 5 or 6 snipped basil leaves, and spread the mixture over the omelette before rolling it.

Smoked salmon omelette with asparagus tips Cook 300 g (10½oz) asparagus spears in boiling salted water for a few minutes until the tips are cooked but still crisp. Drain and refresh in cold water, then cut off the stalks, keeping only the tips. Cut 100 g (3½oz) smoked salmon into wide strips and mix into the beaten eggs just before you cook the omelette. Warm the asparagus tips in 50 g (3½ tbsp) melted butter and fill the omelette before rolling it.

Mussel & chive omelette

SERVES 2

50ml (3½ tbsp) dry white wine

1 thyme sprig

16 fresh mussels, scrubbed

3 tbsp double (heavy) cream

1 tbsp snipped chives

4 eggs

salt and freshly ground pepper

clarified butter (see page 87), optional

Put the wine, thyme and mussels in a small saucepan, cover tightly and cook for a few minutes until the mussels have steamed open. Shell them immediately and place in a bowl, discarding any mussels that have not opened. Strain the juices through a muslin-lined sieve into a small clean pan, to eliminate any sand.

Simmer the mussel juices over a low heat until reduced by half, then add the cream and let it bubble until thick enough to coat the back of a spoon. Turn off the heat, add the chives and mussels, and keep warm (but not hot).

Beat the eggs in a bowl, season lightly and use to make an omelette (see page 122). Half-roll it, then add the creamy mussels and push them into the middle with a spoon. Roll the omelette and slide it on to a warm large plate. To make it look even more appetising, you could brush it with a little clarified butter.

Pear & cinnamon omelette

SERVES 2

1 very ripe large pear, or 2 small pears, 240g (8½oz) total weight

juice of ½ lemon

50g (3½ tbsp) butter

60g (5 tbsp) caster (superfine) sugar

1 tsp ground cinnamon

50ml (3½ tbsp) white wine vinegar

4 eggs

salt and freshly ground pepper

This unusual omelette with 'pickled' pear will surprise and delight your tastebuds. Serve it as an unexpected and harmonious starter.

Peel, halve and core the pear(s), then cut into about 12 segments and toss with the lemon juice.

Melt the butter in a frying pan, add the sugar and cook over a medium heat for about 2 minutes, until the butter and sugar amalgamate and boil to a pale caramel.

Add the pear segments, sprinkle with cinnamon, and cook in the buttery caramel, turning them delicately with a fork every few minutes. When they turn an amber caramel, add the wine vinegar and cook for a further 3 minutes, until the caramel lightly coats the pears. Reserve 4 good segments for the garnish.

Beat the eggs in a bowl, season lightly and use to make an omelette (see page 122). Half-roll it and arrange the pear segments along its length. Roll up the omelette and slide it on to a plate. Arrange the 4 reserved pear segments on top and serve at once.

Rolled Thai omelettes with shrimps on toast croûtes

SERVES 2

1 large egg

1 tsp Thai fish sauce

2 spring onions (scallions)

30g (2 tbsp) softened butter

4 slices of white bread, 1cm (½in) thick

80g (2¾oz) brown shrimps, peeled

pinch of chilli powder

These light, spicy canapés make a perfect prelude to dinner. Plain Thai omelettes are also good rolled up, cut into thin strips and mixed into a rice dish before serving, or added to a chicken broth.

Break the egg into a bowl, add the fish sauce and beat very lightly. Very finely slice the green part of the spring onions; set aside. Shred the top of the white spring onions, keeping the base intact, then immerse in iced water to open out; reserve for the garnish. Drain and pat dry once they have opened.

Gently heat a 20cm (8in) non-stick frying pan with a very flat base, then brush with softened butter. Pour in half of the beaten egg and tilt to spread the egg thinly and evenly over the surface, as if making a crêpe. Cook over a low heat for about 1 minute, until the omelette has set. Remove from the pan and slide on to a sheet of greaseproof paper or a plate. It should be cooked on one side only to keep it soft and malleable. Make another omelette with the rest of the egg in the same way.

To make the croûtes, cut out 4 rounds from each slice of bread, using a 3.5cm (1½in) plain pastry cutter. Toast under the grill (broiler) on one side only.

Scatter the peeled shrimps and green spring onion over the omelettes and sprinkle with the chilli powder. Roll each omelette up delicately but tightly to make an even roll. Cut each one into 8 small slices and stand them upright on the toasted side of the croûtes. Arrange on a serving dish and garnish with the white spring onions.

Thai-style rolled omelette with smoked trout

SERVES 2

200g (7oz) new potatoes

small bunch of watercress, stalks removed

1 filleted smoked trout, about 200g (7oz), skinned

2 large eggs

salt and freshly ground pepper

40g (3½ tbsp) softened butter

5 tbsp olive oil

juice of 3 lemons

2 spring onions (scallions), finely sliced

2 tbsp double (heavy) cream

1 tbsp grated fresh horseradish

Boil the new potatoes in their skins for about 20 minutes until tender, then drain.

Finely shred the watercress leaves, flake the smoked trout and mix them together.

Break the eggs into a bowl, beat them very lightly and season with salt. Gently heat a 20 cm (8in) non-stick frying pan with a very flat base, then brush with a little softened butter. Pour one-quarter of the beaten egg into the pan and tilt to spread the egg thinly and evenly over the surface, as if you were making a crêpe. Cook over a low heat for about 1 minute, until the omelette has set. Remove from the pan and slide on to a sheet of greaseproof paper or a plate. It should be cooked on one side only to keep it soft and malleable. Make three more omelettes in the same way.

Peel the cooked potatoes and grate coarsely. Add the olive oil and the juice of 2 lemons, and season with salt and pepper. Add the spring onions and mix delicately.

Spread the trout and watercress mixture delicately over the omelettes. Mix the cream, remaining lemon juice and the horseradish together, season to taste and drizzle over the trout. Roll up the omelettes gently but firmly and evenly. Divide the potato between 2 plates and arrange 2 omelettes on each plate. Cut the omelettes in half on the diagonal to reveal the filling. Serve as a starter or light lunch.

Spanish tortilla with chorizo

SERVES 4

100 ml (scant 1 cup) olive oil

400 g (14oz) Desirée potatoes, peeled and cubed

2 red onions, roughly chopped

salt and freshly ground pepper

200 g (7oz) chorizo sausage, skinned

1 garlic clove, crushed

2 tbsp chopped flat parsley leaves

6 eggs

A flat tortilla is almost identical to its Italian cousin, the frittata, but is generally thicker and therefore more rustic.

Heat two-thirds of the olive oil in a frying pan, 20–22cm (8–9in) in diameter and about 4cm (1½in) deep. When it is hot, put in the potatoes and cook over a medium heat for 10 minutes. Add the onions, salt lightly, and continue to cook for another 10 minutes or so.

In the meantime, cut the chorizo into 2mm (1⁄16in) slices. Add to the frying pan with the garlic and parsley. Mix well, without crushing the potatoes, and cook for another 2 minutes. Tip everything on to a plate and leave to cool slightly. Wipe out the frying pan with kitchen paper, ready for cooking the tortilla.

Lightly beat the eggs in a large bowl and season with salt and pepper. Heat the remaining olive oil in the frying pan. Using a spoon, mix the eggs delicately into the cooled potato mixture, then pour into the pan. Start cooking over a medium heat, stirring gently every few minutes with the side of a fork, as if making an omelette.

As soon as the eggs are half-cooked, stop stirring, and cook over a very low heat for 2–3 minutes, until the underside of the tortilla is almost cooked. Slide it on to a lightly oiled platter, then invert it back into the pan and cook for another 2 minutes, until both sides are cooked the same and the middle of the tortilla is still soft.

Slide the tortilla on to a plate and serve it whole or cut into wedges. It is equally good served hot, warm or at room temperature, but not chilled.

Frittata of courgettes & confit tomato

SERVES 4

120g (4¼oz) courgettes (zucchini) or patty pan squashes, trimmed

100ml (scant 1 cup) olive oil, plus 2 tbsp to serve

6 eggs

salt and coarsely crushed pepper

200g (7oz) confit tomatoes (see below)

1 small thyme sprig, chopped

8 black olives, stoned (optional)

1 tbsp finely shredded flat parsley leaves

Confit tomatoes

These complement many of my egg dishes. To prepare, peel 200g (7oz) very ripe tomatoes, preferably Roma or Marmande, then halve or quarter and deseed. Heat 250ml (1 cup) light olive oil in a saucepan to 70°C/150°F, then add the tomatoes, 1 halved garlic clove, a pinch of crushed white peppercorns, a thyme sprig and a bay leaf. Cook gently at 70°C/150°F for 10–15 minutes until tender, but not soft. The riper the tomatoes are, the less time they will take.

Leave the tomatoes to cool in the pan, then transfer to a jar or bowl. Cover with cling film (plastic wrap) and keep in the fridge to use as required. Confit tomatoes will keep in the oil for at least 2 weeks. Just season them with salt and pepper before using. If you want to serve the tomatoes warm, place them under a low grill (broiler) briefly, or reheat in a saucepan with a splash of their oil for a few minutes.

This versatile frittata makes a delicious starter, but I sometimes serve it as a main course and simply double up all the ingredients. Cut it into small diamonds to make canapés or tapas packed with Mediterranean flavours.

Cut the courgettes into 1cm (½in) slices or halve the patty pans. Heat two-thirds of the olive oil in a frying pan, 20–22cm (8–9in) in diameter and 4cm (1½in) deep. When it is hot, add the courgettes and cook over a medium heat for 3–4 minutes.

In the meantime, lightly beat the eggs in a bowl and season sparingly with salt and pepper. Add the remaining oil, the confit tomatoes, thyme, and olives if using, to the pan. When everything is very hot, pour in the eggs and cook over a medium heat, stirring gently every few minutes with the side of a fork, as if making an omelette.

As soon as the eggs are half-cooked, stop stirring, and cook over a very low heat for 2–3 minutes, until the underside of the frittata is almost cooked. Slide it on to a lightly oiled plate, then invert it back into the pan and cook for another 2 minutes, still over a low heat, until both sides are cooked the same and the frittata is still soft in the middle. Scatter the parsley over the surface.

Slide the frittata on to a serving plate and cut into wedges. Brush with a little olive oil, and serve some freshly crushed pepper on the side. It is equally good served hot, warm or at room temperature.

Frittata with artichokes & peppers

SERVES 4

6 small, very tender globe
artichokes (the kind you can
eat whole)

180ml (¾ cup) olive oil

juice of 1 lemon

2 red (bell) peppers

1 red onion, chopped

leaves from 1 small thyme sprig

6 eggs

salt and freshly ground pepper

Cut the frittata into wedges, or into small squares to serve as
tapas. It is equally good hot, warm or at room temperature,
but not chilled.

Trim 2cm (¾in) off the tips of the artichoke leaves, and all but 3cm
(1¼in) off the stalks. Peel the attached stalk and remove 2 or 3
outer leaves unless tender. Mix half the olive oil and the lemon
juice in a bowl. Quarter the artichokes and toss in the lemony oil.

Peel the peppers with a vegetable peeler. Quarter, deseed and
remove the pith, then lightly oil the flesh. Heat a griddle pan.
Drain the artichokes and cook on the griddle with the peppers for
1 minute. Give them a quarter-turn and cook for another minute
to mark a lattice. Turn them over and repeat on the other side.
Transfer the peppers to a plate; cook the artichokes for another
2–3 minutes, then remove to the plate.

Heat 2tbsp olive oil in a frying pan, 20–22cm (8–9in) in diameter
and 4cm (1½in) deep. Add the onion and cook for 2 minutes to
soften but not colour. Add the peppers, artichokes and thyme,
moisten with the remaining oil, and heat, stirring, for 3–4 minutes.

Lightly beat the eggs with a very little salt, pour them into the
pan, and cook over a medium heat, stirring gently every few minutes
with the side of a fork, as if making an omelette. As soon as the
eggs are half-cooked, stop stirring, and finish the cooking over a
very low heat for 2–3 minutes, until the underside of the frittata
is almost cooked.

Slide on to a lightly oiled plate, invert back into the pan and cook
gently for another 2 minutes; the frittata should still be soft in the
middle. Slide on to a plate.

Soufflés

Making a soufflé should be a pleasure and ultimately rewarding, but if the idea fills you with dread, here are a few hints for success. The egg whites should be neither too fresh or too cold, or they will not rise very well. I use the whites of medium eggs; if you are unsure of the size, check the volume (see page 12). Don't use a plastic bowl for whisking as plastic retains grease, the enemy of egg whites. Once the whites are half-whisked, add a pinch of salt for savoury soufflés or a little sugar for sweet ones; this will help to maintain their volume. When you fold in the whites, make sure the mixture is hot or warm, never cold or you won't be able to incorporate the whites evenly without overworking. Finally, when the soufflé is in the oven, don't keep opening the door every few minutes – soufflés detest draughts and are likely to collapse!

Classic gruyère soufflés

This technique is similar for all hot soufflés – savoury and sweet.

10 medium egg whites

salt and freshly ground pepper

50g (3½ tbsp) softened butter, to grease dishes

50g (1¾oz) Gruyère, grated, to coat dishes

20g (1½ tbsp) butter

20g (2½ tbsp) plain (all-purpose) flour

250ml (1 cup) milk

pinch of cayenne

6 medium egg yolks

240g (8½oz) Gruyère or Comté, finely grated, plus 8 or 4 thin discs

Preheat the oven to 200°C/400°F/Gas 6. Beat the egg whites with a pinch of salt until soft peaks form.

Generously grease the insides of 8 standard 8 cm (3¼in) ramekins (or four 10 cm/4in soufflé dishes) with the softened butter. Put about 50g (1¾in) grated Gruyère into one dish, rotate it to coat the inside, then tip the excess into another ramekin. Repeat to coat them all.

To make the béchamel, melt the 20 g (1½ tbsp) butter in a pan. Add the flour and cook for 2 minutes, stirring with a whisk, to make a roux. Still stirring, add the cold milk and bring to the boil over a medium heat. Let bubble for a minute or two, then pour the béchamel into a bowl. Season lightly with salt, pepper and cayenne, then whisk in the egg yolks. Cover the bowl with cling film (plastic wrap) and let cool slightly.

Immediately mix one-third of the egg whites into the warm soufflé mixture with a whisk, then, using a large spoon, fold in the rest with one hand while showering in the grated Gruyère with the other. Stop as soon as the mixture is amalgamated.

Spoon the mixture into the ramekins to come 5mm (¼in) above the rim. Smooth the surface with a palette knife, then use a knife tip to ease the mixture away from the side of each ramekin to help it rise.

Stand the ramekins in a deep ovenproof dish lined with a sheet of greaseproof paper and pour in enough almost-boiling water to come halfway up the sides. Bake the soufflés for 4 minutes (or 6 minutes for 10cm/4in dishes). Meanwhile, trim the Gruyère discs to the same diameter as the dishes and cut into 4 segments. Quickly position a segmented Gruyère disc on top of each soufflé and immediately return to the oven for 1 minute (or 2 minutes for 10cm/4in dishes). Put the cooked soufflés on individual plates and serve at once – they won't wait!

These classic soufflés are perfect starters. If I'm serving a three-course meal, I make them in individual 10 cm (4in) soufflé dishes. If they are going to be followed by a number of courses, I use ramekins, which offer just 4 or 5 delicious mouthfuls. Comté cheese has a fuller, stronger flavour than Gruyère and can be used instead. The choice is yours.

For all sweet soufflés (chocolate, vanilla, mango, etc), whisk the egg whites with a pinch of sugar rather than a pinch of salt.

I always allow generous quantities of mixture for my individual soufflés, so don't worry if you have some left over after filling the ramekins – better safe than sorry!

Roquefort & walnut soufflés

Follow the recipe for classic Gruyère soufflés, coating the dishes with fine white breadcrumbs rather than grated cheese. Replace the 240g (8½oz) Gruyère or Comté with 160g (5¾oz) chilled Roquefort, cut into small pieces. (This should not be too soft or over-ripe.) Fold into the béchamel with the egg whites, then fold in 12 coarsely chopped walnuts, and finally 4 finely diced fresh, very ripe figs. Bake as directed (see above) and serve immediately, with a salad of mâche (lamb's lettuce) and thick batons of apple (preferably Granny Smith), dressed with a well-seasoned vinaigrette.

Cheddar, sorrel & anchovy soufflés

Makes 4

50g (3½ tbsp) softened butter, to grease dishes

200g (7oz) Cheddar, finely grated, plus 50g (1¾oz) to coat dishes and 20g (⅔oz) to finish

20g (1½ tbsp) butter

20g (2½ tbsp) plain (all-purpose) flour

250ml (1 cup) milk

salt and freshly ground pepper

6 medium egg yolks

1 tbsp anchovy essence

10 medium egg whites

15g (½oz) sorrel leaves, de-stalked and shredded

4 anchovy fillets in oil, drained

The creamy texture of this soufflé conceals a surprise element – the shredded sorrel. Its slight acidity is a perfect foil for the anchovies. When sorrel is not in season, use spinach instead.

Butter 4 individual 10 cm (4in) soufflé dishes and coat the insides with 50g (1¾oz) of the grated cheese.

To make the béchamel, melt the butter in a small pan, add the flour and cook, stirring, for 2 minutes. Still stirring, add the milk and bring to the boil over a medium heat. Let bubble for a minute or two, then pour into a bowl. Season very lightly with salt and plenty of pepper, and whisk in the egg yolks, then the anchovy essence. Cover the bowl with cling film (plastic wrap); let cool slightly.

Preheat the oven to 200°C/400°F/Gas 6. Beat the egg whites with a pinch of salt until soft peaks form. Immediately mix one-third of the egg whites into the warm soufflé mixture with a whisk, then, using a large spoon, fold in the rest with one hand while showering in the sorrel and 200 g (7oz) grated Cheddar with the other. Stop as soon as the mixture is completely amalgamated.

Spoon the mixture into the soufflé dishes to come 5mm (¼in) above the rim. Bake the soufflés for 6 minutes, then sprinkle the tops with a little grated Cheddar and immediately return to the oven for a further 2 minutes. Top each soufflé with a rolled anchovy fillet and serve immediately.

Bacon & parsley soufflés with eggs 'en surprise'

50g (3½oz) softened butter,
to grease dishes

50g (1¾oz) Gruyère or Comté,
grated,
to coat dishes

20g (1½ tbsp) butter

20g (2½ tbsp) plain (all-purpose)
flour

250ml (1 cup) milk

salt and freshly ground pepper

6 medium egg yolks

160g (5¾oz) bacon, thinly sliced,
cut into 5mm (¼in) wide lardons

1 tbsp groundnut oil

8 medium egg whites

20g (⅔oz) flat parsley leaves,
finely snipped

4 poached eggs (see page 42)

These little soufflés are ideal for lunch or brunch. The mingling of the yolk from the surprise poached egg with the soufflé is a treat. A tomato coulis on the side goes well, but it is not essential.

Butter 4 individual 10 cm (4in) soufflé dishes and coat the insides with grated cheese.

To make the béchamel, melt the butter in a small pan, add the flour and cook, stirring, for 2 minutes. Still stirring, add the milk and bring to the boil over a medium heat. Let bubble for a minute or two, then pour into a bowl. Season lightly, then whisk in the egg yolks. Cover the bowl with cling film (plastic wrap); let cool slightly.

Put the lardons in a saucepan, cover with water, bring to the boil and boil for 30 seconds. Remove, refresh, drain well and pat dry. Heat the oil in a non-stick frying pan and brown the lardons over a high heat for 1 minute, then drain and set aside.

Preheat the oven to 200°C/400°F/Gas 6. Beat the egg whites with a pinch of salt until soft peaks form. Immediately mix one-third into the warm soufflé mixture with a whisk, then, using a large spoon, fold in the rest with one hand while showering in the lardons and parsley with the other. Stop as soon as the mixture is amalgamated.

Heat the poached eggs in boiling water for 30 seconds, then drain well. Two-thirds fill the soufflé dishes with the soufflé mixture. Carefully place a poached egg in the centre of each dish, then fill up with mixture to come 5mm (¼in) above the rim. Stand the dishes in a bain-marie. Cook for 8 minutes, then serve immediately.

Langoustine soufflés with shellfish coulis

A springtime speciality at The Waterside Inn, these soufflés are immensely popular and certainly merit the time taken to prepare them ... once tasted, never forgotten.

MAKES 8

8 fine langoustines

salt and freshly ground pepper

2 tbsp groundnut oil

4 button mushrooms, sliced

3 shallots, very thinly sliced

2 tarragon sprigs

600ml (2½ cups) ready-made fish stock (bought fresh stock is fine)

50g (3½ tbsp) softened butter, to grease dishes

20g (1½ tbsp) butter

20g (2½ tbsp) plain (all-purpose) flour

pinch of cayenne

4 medium egg yolks

75ml (5 tbsp) double (heavy) cream

1 tbsp Cognac or Armagnac (optional)

8 medium egg whites

Add the langoustines to a pan of boiling salted water and cook for 4 minutes. Drain and shell the langoustines when they are cool enough to handle. Cut the tail meat into 1cm (½in) pieces, place in a bowl and cover with cling film (plastic wrap). Split the heads lengthways with a heavy knife and use for the stock.

Heat the oil in a saucepan, add the langoustine heads and cook over a medium heat to colour them, stirring every minute. Add the mushrooms, shallots and tarragon, and sweat gently for 5 minutes. Add the fish stock and cook over a medium heat until reduced almost by half. Pass the stock through a chinois, pushing with the back of a ladle to extract as much flavour as you can from the langoustine heads. Put the stock to one side to cool slightly.

Butter the insides of 8 deep 8 cm (3¼in) ramekins, about 6cm (2½in) high. Melt the butter in a small saucepan, add the flour and cook for 2 minutes, stirring constantly with a whisk, to make a roux. Still stirring, add just 220ml (scant 1 cup) of the langoustine stock and bring to the boil over a medium heat. Let it bubble gently for a minute or two, then pour into a bowl. Season lightly with salt and a pinch of cayenne, and whisk in the egg yolks. Cover the bowl with cling film (plastic wrap) and leave to cool slightly.

To make the shellfish coulis, put the rest of the langoustine stock into a small saucepan and bring to the boil. Immediately add the cream, and the Cognac if using, and let bubble for 2 minutes, then season with salt and pepper to taste; keep hot.

Preheat the oven to 200°C/400°F/Gas 6. Beat the egg whites with a pinch of salt until soft peaks form. Immediately mix one-third into the warm soufflé mixture with a whisk, then, using a large spoon, fold in the rest until evenly incorporated. Half-fill the ramekins with the mixture. Gently warm the langoustine tails and divide them between the dishes, then fill up with soufflé mixture to come 5mm (¼in) above the rim.

Stand the ramekins in a deep ovenproof dish lined with a sheet of greaseproof paper and pour in enough almost-boiling water to come halfway up the sides. Bake for 6 minutes until well risen and golden.

Take these very light and delicate soufflés to the table straight from the oven. Make a little slit in the middle with a knife tip and pour in the hot langoustine coulis to serve.

Chocolate soufflés

40 g (3 tbsp) softened butter, to grease dishes

40 g (3¼ tbsp) caster (superfine) sugar, plus 40 g (3¼ tbsp) to coat dishes

15 g (2 tbsp) cocoa powder, sifted

120 g (4¼oz) plain chocolate (70% cocoa solids), chopped into small pieces

10 medium egg whites

icing (confectioners') sugar, to dust

For the pastry cream

350 ml (1½ cups) milk

80 g (6½ tbsp) caster (superfine) sugar

4 medium egg yolks

30 g (3½ tbsp) plain (all-purpose) flour

These are heavenly! To make them even more divine, slip a spoonful of freshly churned vanilla ice cream (see page 224) into the centre of each soufflé at the table.

Butter 4 individual 10 cm (4in) soufflé dishes and coat the insides with 40 g (3¼ tbsp) of the sugar.

To make the pastry cream, put the milk and two-thirds of the sugar in a small pan and slowly bring to the boil. Put the egg yolks and remaining sugar in a bowl and whisk to a ribbon consistency, then incorporate the flour. Pour the hot milk on to the yolks, stirring continuously with a whisk. Return to the pan and whisk over a low heat for 1 minute. Pour into a bowl, cover with cling film (plastic wrap) and let cool slightly.

Preheat the oven to 190°C/375°F/Gas 5 and put a baking sheet inside to heat. Measure 280 g (1¼ cups) of the pastry cream and delicately mix in the cocoa powder and chopped chocolate using a whisk. (Keep the rest of the pastry cream for another use.)

Beat the egg whites to a thick foam, then add the remaining 40 g (3¼ tbsp) sugar and continue to beat until they form soft peaks. Fold one-third into the pastry cream using a whisk, then delicately fold in the rest with a large spoon; the mixture will be fairly loose.

Divide the mixture between the soufflé dishes, filling them to the top. Stand on the hot baking sheet and cook for 10 minutes. As you take the soufflés out of the oven, dust the tops with icing sugar, place on warm plates and serve immediately.

Vanilla & mango soufflés with passion fruit coulis

SERVES 4

40g (3 tbsp) softened butter, to grease dishes

80g (6½ tbsp) caster (superfine) sugar, plus 40g (3¼ tbsp) to coat dishes

8 medium egg whites

1 very ripe mango, about 400g (14oz), peeled, stoned and finely diced

For the pastry cream

350ml milk (1½ cups)

70g caster (superfine) sugar (heaped ⅓ cup)

1 vanilla pod, split lengthways

7 medium egg yolks

50g (6 tbsp) plain (all-purpose) flour

For the passion fruit coulis

30g (2½ tbsp) caster (superfine) sugar

juice of 2 oranges

2 passion fruit, halved

Cut the frittata into wedges, or into small squares to serve as tapas. It is equally good hot, warm or at room temperature, but not chilled.

Butter 4 individual 10 cm (4in) soufflé dishes and coat the insides with the sugar.

To make the coulis, boil the sugar and orange juice until reduced by one-third, pour into a bowl and let cool. Scrape the passion fruit seeds into the cold syrup; set aside.

For the pastry cream, put the milk and 40g (3¼ tbsp) sugar in a small pan, scrape in the seeds from the vanilla pod and slowly bring to the boil. Whisk the egg yolks and remaining 30g (2½ tbsp) sugar in a bowl to a ribbon consistency, then incorporate the flour. Pour the hot milk on to the yolks, stirring continuously with a whisk. Return to the pan and whisk over a low heat for 1 minute, then pour into a bowl, cover with cling film (plastic wrap) and cool slightly.

Preheat the oven to 200°C/400°F/Gas 6 and put a baking sheet inside to heat. Beat the egg whites to a thick foam, then add the 80g (6½ tbsp) sugar and continue to beat until they form soft peaks. Fold one-third into the pastry cream using a whisk, then delicately fold in the rest with a large spoon, scattering in the diced mango as you go.

Divide the mixture between the soufflé dishes, to come level with the rim. Stand on the hot baking sheet and cook for 8 minutes. Serve the soufflés as soon as they come out of the oven on warm plates, with the coulis in a sauceboat. Invite guests to make a small well in the middle of their soufflé with a little spoon and pour in a little coulis.

Crêpes & Batters

Fortunately, my mother was an excellent cook who loved making crêpes for us. Shortly after the war, when I was quite small, she would make a batter with the few eggs she had, lots of flour to fill us up, and milk diluted with water. The resulting crêpes were very thick to keep us sustained, but as things improved over the years, they became finer and finer, until almost like lace. Nowadays, I love making crêpes and waffles for my grandchildren. They all help to prepare the batter and join in with the cooking. Today, crêperies are everywhere, offering pancakes made from different flours like buckwheat or rye, and enclosing a myriad of savoury and sweet fillings. Batters can be made a day in advance and kept in an airtight container in the fridge until needed. From fritters to Yorkshire puddings and clafoutis, they offer a palette of different textures.

Crêpes

SERVES 4 OR 8

125g (scant 1 cup) plain (all-purpose) flour

15g (1½ tbsp) caster (superfine) sugar

pinch of salt

2 eggs

325ml (1⅓ cups) milk

100ml (scant ½ cup) double (heavy) cream

few drops of vanilla extract or orange flower water, or a little grated lemon zest

20g (1½ tbsp) clarified butter (see page 87), to cook

Roll up the crêpes, or fold in half or into quarters and eat immediately, either just as they are, dusted with sugar, or filled.

To make the batter, put the flour, sugar and salt in a bowl. Add the eggs, mix well with a whisk, then stir in 100ml (scant ½ cup) milk to make a smooth batter. Gradually stir in the rest of the milk and the cream. Leave the batter to rest in a warm place for about an hour.

When you are ready to cook the crêpes, give the batter a stir and flavour with vanilla, orange flower water or lemon zest. Brush a 22cm (9in) crêpe pan with a little clarified butter and heat. Ladle in a little batter and tilt the pan to cover the base thinly. Cook the crêpe for about 1 minute.

As soon as little holes appear all over the surface, turn the crêpe over and cook the other side for 30–40 seconds. Transfer to a plate and cook the rest of the batter, stacking the crêpes interleaved with greaseproof paper as they are cooked.

Crêpes with summer berries

Serves 6

1 quantity crêpe batter (see page 154)

150g (5½oz) raspberries

150g (5½oz) blackberries

6 small mint sprigs

icing (confectioners') sugar, to dust

For the red berry coulis

50g (¼ cup) sugar

200g (7oz) raspberries or strawberries

juice of ½ lemon

First make the red berry coulis. Put the sugar and 50ml (3½ tbsp) water in a saucepan and set over a low heat until the sugar has dissolved. Increase the heat and boil the sugar syrup for 3 minutes, then remove and leave to cool. When cold, put the sugar syrup in a blender with the berries and lemon juice, and whiz for 1 minute, then pass the coulis through a chinois into a bowl.

Cook the crêpes (see page 154). Put a warm crêpe on each plate and scatter on some raspberries and blackberries. Cover with another crêpe and partially fold it back over itself. Spoon on little dabs of red berry coulis, add a sprig of mint, dust with icing sugar and serve at once.

Put the remaining crêpes, berries and red berry coulis on the table for people to help themselves.

Illustrated on previous page

Crêpes with apples & candied kumquats

SERVES 4

2 cooking apples, preferably Bramleys

30g (2 tbsp) butter

8 candied kumquats (see page 259)

4 warm crêpes (see page 154)

icing (confectioners') sugar, to dust

I like to serve these tempting crêpes with a vanilla crème anglaise (see page 202) for an indulgent treat.

Prepare the filling before you cook the crêpes. Peel and core the apples, cut into segments and put in a saucepan with the butter and 50ml (3½ tbsp) water. Stew until soft, then purée using a hand-held blender to make a smooth compote.

Cut the kumquats into 2–3mm (⅟₁₆in) thick rounds and mix them into the warm apple compote. Spread over the middle of the crêpes, then roll them up.

Put a filled crêpe on each warm plate and dust lightly with icing sugar. Serve at once.

Savoury crêpes with seasonal crudités

150g (5½oz) carrots, grated

50g (1¾oz) red onion or shallots, chopped

50g (⅓ cup) sultanas (golden raisins)

30g (¼ cup) pine nuts, toasted

2 hard-boiled eggs (see page 18), chopped

2 tbsp snipped flat parsley leaves, plus 1–2 tsp snipped for the batter

5 tbsp groundnut oil

2 tbsp wine vinegar

salt and freshly ground pepper

½ quantity crêpe batter (see page 154), without sugar or flavourings

lemon wedges

To vary the filling, replace the carrot with freshly grated celeriac or beetroot.

First prepare the filling. Mix the grated carrot with the chopped onion. Blanch the sultanas in boiling water for 10 seconds, then refresh in cold water and drain well. Add to the carrot mixture with the toasted pine nuts and mix well.

Flavour the chopped hard-boiled eggs with the 2 tbsp snipped parsley.

Whisk the oil with the wine vinegar and seasoning to make a vinaigrette. Toss the carrot mixture in the vinaigrette. Check the seasoning.

Flavour the crêpe batter with a little snipped parsley, then cook 8 crêpes (see page 154). Arrange a crêpe on each of 4 plates. Spread the carrot mixture on top, cover each with another crêpe and sprinkle the chopped egg on top. Serve cold, with lemon wedges.

Chicken & mushroom crêpes

SERVES 4

2 boneless chicken breasts, 150–200g (5½–7oz) each

200ml (scant 1 cup) chicken stock

40g (3 tbsp) butter

150g (5½oz) small button mushrooms, sliced

juice of ½ lemon

salt and freshly ground pepper

4 tbsp snipped flat parsley leaves (optional), plus 1–2 tsp for the batter

1 quantity freshly made Mornay sauce (see page 282)

½ quantity crêpe batter (see page 154), without sugar or flavourings

First make the filling. Remove the skins from the chicken breasts and place them in a pan. Pour on the chicken stock and bring to a simmer. Lower the heat and poach gently for 10 minutes (the stock should barely tremble). Leave the chicken to cool in the liquor.

Melt the butter in a frying pan, add the mushrooms and cook over a medium heat for 2–3 minutes. Add the lemon juice, season with salt and pepper, and scatter over the parsley if using. Transfer to a bowl.

Cut the chicken breasts into thick strips and mix with the mushrooms. Tip the mixture into the hot Mornay sauce, stir and adjust the seasoning.

Flavour the crêpe batter with a little snipped parsley, then cook 4 crêpes (see page 154), each about 26 cm (10½in) diameter and a touch thicker than usual.

Put a warm crêpe on each warmed plate. Divide the filling between the crêpes, spooning it more generously on to the part furthest from you. Fold over the sides to form a cornet shape. Serve with a mâche (lamb's lettuce) salad on the side.

Waffles

SERVES 6

For the waffle batter

160g (scant 1¼ cups) plain (all-purpose) flour

15g (1½ tbsp) caster (superfine) sugar, plus an extra pinch

pinch of salt

50g (3½ tbsp) butter, melted

2 eggs, separated

270ml (scant 1¼ cups) milk

few drops of vanilla extract or orange flower water, or a little grated lemon zest

To cook and serve

20g (1½ tbsp) butter, softened

icing (confectioners') or caster (superfine) sugar, to dust, or honey or maple syrup

Everyone loves waffles, but you will need a waffle iron to make your own. For a decadent finish, top with ice cream or a generous spoonful of Chiboust cream (see page 207) and blueberries.

To make the waffle batter, combine the flour, sugar, salt, melted butter, egg yolks and about one-third of the milk in a bowl. Whisk lightly until smooth, then gradually whisk in the rest of the milk. Add your chosen flavouring, cover the bowl with cling film (plastic wrap) and set aside while you heat the waffle iron (for 5–10 minutes before cooking).

In a small bowl, whisk the egg whites with a pinch of sugar to a thick foam (but not to peaks). Gently fold into the waffle batter, using a balloon whisk.

Lightly brush the waffle iron with softened butter, then ladle in enough batter to cover the griddle. Close the lid and cook for 3–4 minutes, until the waffles are cooked to your liking. Some like them dry and crisp; others soft and lightly coloured. Cook the rest of the batter in the same way. Don't bother to grease the waffle iron each time; you only need to do this every third or fourth waffle.

Serve the waffles immediately on warm plates or a large platter. Dust with icing or caster sugar, or drizzle with a little honey or maple syrup.

Cherry clafoutis

SERVES 8

100g (7 tbsp) butter

350g (12oz) ripe cherries, stoned

For the batter

2 eggs

80g (scant ⅔ cup) plain
(all-purpose) flour

80g (⅓ cup) butter, melted and
cooled

60g (5 tbsp) granulated sugar,
plus extra to dust

150ml (scant ⅔ cup) cold milk

1 vanilla pod, split lengthways

1 tbsp kirsch (optional)

You can use other soft-fleshed seasonal fruits, such as greengages, mirabelles, blackberries and pears. A spoonful of appropriate eau-de-vie or liqueur is the cherry on the cake.

To make the batter, very lightly beat the eggs in a bowl with a fork and add the flour. Whisk in the melted butter, then gradually mix in the granulated sugar and milk. Use a knife tip to scrape the vanilla seeds into the batter, and add the kirsch if using.

Preheat the oven to 200°C/400°F/Gas 6. Use 60g (¼ cup) of the butter to generously grease a 20cm (8in) diameter, 5cm (2in) deep ovenproof dish. Spread the cherries in the bottom, then pour the batter over them.

Carefully place in the hot oven, making sure that the batter doesn't spill over the top. Bake for 10 minutes, then lower the oven setting to 180°C/350°F/Gas 4. Cut the remaining butter into small pieces, dot them over the top of the clafoutis and bake for another 25 minutes or so.

To check if the clafoutis is cooked, delicately slide in a knife tip. If it comes out smooth and clean, the clafoutis is ready. Dust with a little granulated sugar and leave to stand for a few minutes. Serve the clafoutis warm, from the dish.

Illustrated on previous page

Apple & pear fritters

SERVES 4

5g (⅛oz) fresh yeast

600ml (2½ cups) milk

100g (¾ cup) plain (all-purpose) flour

50ml (3½ tbsp) light beer

1 egg yolk

pinch of salt

1 tbsp groundnut oil

1 apple, preferably Cox's

1 pear, preferably Comice

juice of 1 lemon

To cook and serve

groundnut oil, to deep-fry

1½ medium egg whites

pinch of caster (superfine) sugar, plus extra to dust

Dip these sweet fritters into a red berry coulis (see page 158) and they are even more tempting. Other fruits, such as bananas and pineapple, also make excellent fritters.

To make the fritter batter, whisk the yeast with half of the milk in a small bowl. Combine the flour, beer, the remaining milk, egg yolk and salt in a large bowl and whisk lightly until smooth. Pour in the yeast liquid and the 1 tbsp oil, mix well, then cover with cling film (plastic wrap) and leave to stand for 2 hours.

Peel the apple and pear, cut each into 8 or 10 segments, removing the core, and sprinkle with lemon juice.

Heat the oil for deep-frying in a suitable pan to 170°C/325°F. In a small bowl, whisk the egg whites with a pinch of sugar to a thick foam (but not to peaks), then delicately fold into the batter, using a spatula.

Cook the fritters in batches. One at a time, lift the apple segments with a fork, dip into the batter to coat, then drop them into the hot oil. Deep-fry for 3–4 minutes until lightly coloured, turning them over with the tip of the fork prongs to colour both sides; the fritters will rise to the surface when they are cooked.

Remove and drain on kitchen paper. Cook the pear segments in the same way, allowing 2–3 minutes cooking only, as these are more tender than the apples. Serve the fritters as soon as they are all cooked, but take care – they will be very hot. Sprinkle with caster sugar as you serve them.

Seafood & monkfish fritters

SERVES 4

100g (¾ cup) plain (all-purpose) flour

50ml (3½ tbsp) white wine vinegar

1 medium egg

salt and freshly ground pepper

8 large raw prawns (jumbo shrimp)

1 squid, about 200g (7oz), cleaned

4 monkfish medallions, about 75g (2½oz) each

To cook and serve

groundnut oil, to deep-fry

1 lemon, cut into quarters

mayonnaise (see pages 266–9, optional)

This light, crunchy fritter batter is perfect for seafood and fish, as it provides a delicate coating.

To make the fritter batter, put the flour in a bowl, then add 100ml (scant ½ cup) cold water, the wine vinegar and egg, and mix with a whisk. Season with a very little salt and pepper. Cover with cling film (plastic wrap) and leave to stand for 20 minutes.

Shell the prawn tails, leaving the heads attached. Cut the squid pouch into rings, rinse and pat dry. Do not rinse the monkfish medallions, but pat them dry.

To cook the fritters, heat the oil in a suitable pan to 180°C/350°F. Deep-fry the fish in batches. One at a time, lift the squid rings with a fork, dunk them into the batter to coat, then drop into the hot oil and fry for 2 minutes. As soon as the fritters are cooked, lift them out with a slotted spoon or strainer and drain on kitchen paper.

Repeat with the monkfish medallions, allowing 3–4 minutes deep-frying.

Hold the prawn heads in your fingers near the antennae, and dip only the tails into the batter. Put them into the hot oil carefully so that it doesn't splutter and deep-fry for about 2 minutes.

Serve the fritters straightaway, with lemon wedges. You might also like to serve a mayonnaise on the side for dipping.

Yorkshires with caramelised onions & chipolatas

Serves 6

For the Yorkshire batter

2 eggs

70g (½ cup) plain (all-purpose) flour

200ml (scant 1 cup) semi-skimmed milk

salt and freshly ground pepper

For the filling

80g (⅓ cup) butter

1 large onion, about 300g (10½oz), very thinly sliced

100ml (scant ½ cup) beef dripping or groundnut oil

2 tbsp clarified butter (see page 87) or groundnut oil

18 small chipolatas, blanched

pinch of sugar

To make the batter, lightly whisk the eggs in a bowl, then whisk in the flour a little at a time, until smooth. Slowly add the milk, stirring with the whisk, and season with a little salt and pepper. Cover and refrigerate the batter for at least 2 hours.

Preheat the oven to 220°C/425°F/Gas 7. For the filling, melt the butter in a small pan and gently cook the onion for 30 minutes, stirring every 5 minutes, until meltingly soft.

Meanwhile, put a little dripping or oil into each of 6 Yorkshire pudding moulds and place in the oven for 4–5 minutes until the fat starts to smoke. Give the batter a stir, then ladle it into the moulds until it almost reaches the top. Bake for 25 minutes or until the puddings are golden brown and crisp, but still slightly soft in the middle.

In the meantime, heat the clarified butter or oil in a frying pan and cook the chipolatas for 3–4 minutes until golden; keep warm.

Sprinkle the onion with the sugar, increase the heat slightly and cook, stirring, until lightly caramelised.

Unmould the Yorkshire puddings on to a wire rack, taking care not to burn yourself, then place one on each warm plate. Fill the cavities with the caramelised onion and chipolatas. Serve piping hot.

Egg-rich Pastry & Pasta

Egg-rich pastries form the basis of delicious quiches, tarts and tartlets. To ensure that the pastry cases are baked to perfection, the flan pastry must be rolled out as thinly as possible – a 2–3mm (¹⁄₁₆in) thickness is ideal. A thick, undercooked case will ruin a tart, however delicious the filling. Choux paste is mainly associated with desserts but it also forms the basis of mouth-watering gougères (see page 178), which I serve as canapés at The Waterside Inn. Pasta is quick and simple to make and cut, using a pasta machine, and tastes far better than commercial varieties. If you do not already own a pasta machine, I strongly recommend you buy one. Everyone loves pasta, and you can create an endless variety of tempting meals, by flavouring it with tender vegetables, seafood, cheese and fresh herbs, or serving it alla carbonara (see page 198).

Choux pastry

Makes 40–50 little buns

125ml (½ cup) milk

100g (7 tbsp) butter, diced

½ tsp salt

1 tsp sugar

150g (heaped 1 cup) plain (all-purpose) flour

4 medium eggs

eggwash (1 egg beaten with 1 tbsp milk)

Combine the milk, 125ml (½ cup) water, the butter, salt and sugar in a saucepan and set over a low heat. Bring to the boil and immediately take the pan off the heat. Shower in the flour and beat the mixture with a wooden spoon until smooth.

Return the pan to a medium heat for about 1 minute, stirring constantly, to dry out the paste. Tip it into a bowl.

Add the eggs one by one, beating with the wooden spoon. Once they are all incorporated into the mixture, it should be smooth and shiny, and thick enough to pipe. The choux paste is now ready to use. (If you are not using it immediately, brush the surface with eggwash to prevent a crust forming.)

Pipe small mounds on to a baking sheet lined with greaseproof paper in staggered rows, using a piping bag fitted with a 1cm (½in) nozzle. Brush with eggwash and lightly mark the tops with the back of a fork. Bake at 200°C/400°F/Gas 6 for 15–20 minutes until dry and crisp, but still soft inside. Cool on a wire rack.

Choux buns with coffee & drambuie mousse

SERVES 8-10

1 quantity choux pastry (see page 174)

100ml (scant ½ cup) whipping cream

20g (1½ tbsp) caster (superfine) sugar

½ quantity (375g/13oz) crème pâtissière (see page 206), cooled

4 tbsp instant coffee powder, dissolved in 2 tbsp warm water

75ml (5 tbsp) Drambuie, or to taste

To finish

icing (confectioners') sugar

cocoa powder

These little choux buns make a lovely dessert, but I also like to serve them as a teatime treat.

Preheat the oven to 200°C/400°F/Gas 6. Make the choux pastry, and shape and cook the buns following the method on page 174. Cool on a wire rack.

To make the mousse, whip the cream with the sugar to a ribbon consistency and fold into the cooled crème pâtissière, then fold in the coffee and Drambuie.

Make a small opening in the side of each choux bun with the tip of a knife. Using a piping bag fitted with a plain 5mm (¼in) nozzle, pipe a generous amount of coffee mousse into each bun.

To serve, dust half the choux buns with a little icing sugar and the rest with cocoa powder. Arrange on individual plates or a platter, allowing about 5 per person.

Gougères

1 quantity choux pastry (see page 174)

100g Gruyère or Comté, grated

pinch of cayenne

small pinch of freshly grated nutmeg

a little sweet paprika, to dust (optional)

These little gougères are usually offered at the end of a wine tasting in Burgundy wine cellars. They make good canapés, or you can serve them filled with Mornay sauce (see page 282) as a warm starter.

Preheat the oven to 200°C/400°F/Gas 6. Make the choux pastry following the method on page 174. When the last egg has been incorporated and the mixture is very smooth, stir in three-quarters of the grated cheese, the cayenne and nutmeg. Take care not to overwork the mixture.

Pipe the choux paste on to a baking sheet lined with greaseproof paper in staggered rows, using a piping bag fitted with a 1cm (½in) nozzle. Brush with eggwash, then mark the tops lightly with the back of a fork and sprinkle with the rest of the cheese. Bake for 15–20 minutes until dry and crisp on the outside, but still soft inside. Immediately transfer to a wire rack.

Serve the gougères warm, just as they are, or dusted with sweet paprika.

Flan pastry

250g (heaped 1¾ cups) plain (all-purpose) flour

125g (½ cup) butter, diced and slightly softened

1 medium egg

1 tsp salt

2 tsp caster (superfine) sugar

This dough makes the perfect shell for tarts, tartlets and quiche.

First, put the flour in a mound on a work surface (preferably marble) and make a well in the middle. Put the butter, egg, salt and sugar into the well. Using your fingertips, mix all the ingredients in the well together, then gradually draw in the flour, little by little.

Mix until all the ingredients are almost amalgamated and the pastry has a slightly sandy texture. Add 40ml (2½ tbsp) cold water and incorporate, using your fingertips.

Knead the pastry 2 or 3 times with the heel of your hand to make it completely smooth. Roll it into a ball, wrap in cling film (plastic wrap) and rest in the fridge for 1–2 hours before using.

Pâte sucrée

Makes 520g

250g (heaped 1¾ cups) plain (all-purpose) flour

100g (7 tbsp) butter, diced and slightly softened

100g (¾ cup) icing (confectioners') sugar

small pinch of salt

2 medium eggs

This sweet pastry is relatively easy to work with and is perfect for blind-baked tarts and tartlets. It is made in the same way as flan pastry (see left) and – like flan pastry – it keeps well in the fridge for several days, or it can be frozen.

Put the flour on a work surface (preferably marble) and make a well. Put in the butter, icing sugar and salt.

Using your fingertips, mix all the ingredients in the well, then add the eggs and gradually draw in the flour, little by little, and mix well.

When everything is completely amalgamated, knead the pastry 2 or 3 times with the heel of your hand to make it completely smooth, wrap it in cling film (plastic wrap) and rest in the fridge for 1–2 hours before using.

Lining a tart tin & baking blind

Roll out the pastry on a clean, smooth surface (preferably marble) and keep dusting it with a veil of flour. Give the pastry a quarter-turn each time you roll it to keep the shape as round as possible.

When you achieve the required thickness, lightly roll the pastry round the rolling pin, and carefully unroll it over a flan ring or tart tin. Use your thumb and index finger to push the pastry into the base and side of the mould.

Cut off the excess pastry by rolling the rolling pin across the rim of the mould, then pinch up the edges with your thumb and index finger to crimp them about 5mm (¼in) above the rim. Refrigerate the tart case for at least 20 minutes before baking.

Prick the bottom of the pastry case in 5 or 6 places with a fork. Line it with greaseproof paper and fill with baking beans or dried pulses. Bake at 200–220°C/400–425°F/Gas 6–7 for about 20 minutes.

Remove the baking beans and paper and return the pastry case to the oven for a final 10–15 minutes, depending on the type of pastry and its thickness.

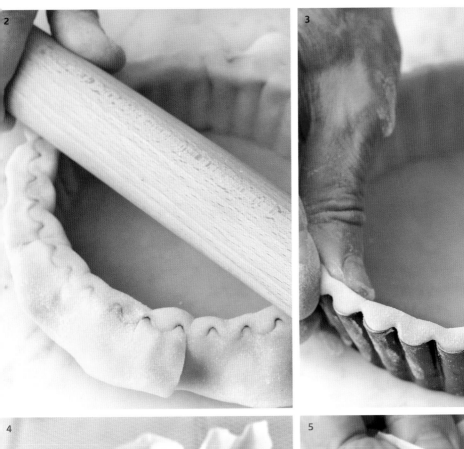

Quiche lorraine

SERVES 8–10

350g (12oz) flan pastry (see page 180)

20g (1½ tbsp) butter, to grease

flour, to dust

40g (1½oz) Gruyère or Comté, cut into thin flakes, to finish

For the filling

200g (7oz) salt pork belly, derinded and cut into small lardons

1 tbsp groundnut oil

200g (7oz) Gruyère or Comté, coarsely grated

3 medium eggs

6 medium egg yolks

600ml (2½ cups) double (heavy) cream

salt and freshly ground pepper

pinch of freshly grated nutmeg

2 tbsp kirsch (optional)

This recipe is for a large classic quiche, but you can make individual ones if you prefer, adjusting the cooking time accordingly.

For the pastry case, grease a 22cm (8½in) flan ring (3cm/1¼in deep) and place on a baking sheet in the fridge. Roll out the pastry into a round about 3mm (⅛in) thick and use to line the flan ring (see page 182). Rest in the fridge for 20 minutes. Preheat the oven to 200°C/400°F/Gas 6.

Prick the bottom of the pastry case, line with greaseproof paper and baking beans or dried pulses and bake blind for 20 minutes. Remove the beans and paper and leave to cool in the ring. Increase the oven setting to 220°C/425°F/Gas 7.

For the filling, blanch the lardons in boiling water, refresh in cold water, drain and dry. Heat the oil in a non-stick frying pan and brown the lardons over a medium heat for 1 minute; drain. Scatter in the pastry case, then sprinkle on the grated cheese.

Lightly whisk the whole eggs, yolks and cream in a bowl. Season with salt, pepper and nutmeg, then add the kirsch if using. Pour into the pastry case and bake for 20 minutes. Lower the oven setting to 200°C/400°F/Gas 6 and cook for another 15 minutes. Scatter the cheese flakes over the surface and bake for a final 5 minutes.

Immediately slide the quiche on to a wire rack, using a large palette knife. Gently lift the flan ring off. Serve the quiche warm or tepid, but not piping hot.

Leek flamiche

SERVES 8–10

350g (12oz) flan pastry (see page 180)

20g (1½ tbsp) butter, to grease

flour, to dust

For the filling

1kg (1lb 2oz) leeks, trimmed, split lengthways and well washed

60g (¼ cup) butter

salt and freshly ground pepper

100ml (scant ½ cup) double (heavy) cream

5 medium egg yolks

15g (1½ tbsp) Madras curry powder (optional)

The curry adds a special something to this flan from the Champagne region of France. Perhaps surprisingly, it enhances rather than detracts from the flavour of the leeks.

For the filling, cut the leeks into 5mm (¼in) slices. Melt the butter in a pan, add the leeks, season with a little salt and pepper, then cover and sweat gently for 20–30 minutes until tender, stirring occasionally. Transfer to a bowl and leave to cool completely.

For the pastry case, grease a 22cm (8½in) flan ring (3cm/1¼in deep), and place on a baking sheet in the fridge. Roll out the pastry into a round about 3mm (⅛in) thick and use to line the flan ring (see page 182). Leave to rest in the fridge for at least 20 minutes. Preheat the oven to 200°C/400°F/Gas 6.

Prick the bottom of the pastry case, line with greaseproof paper and baking beans or dried pulses and bake blind for 20 minutes. Remove the beans and paper and leave to cool in the ring.

To make the filling, whip the cream very lightly with the egg yolks and curry powder if using, then fold in the cooled leeks. Adjust the seasoning if necessary. Pour the leek mixture into the pastry case and bake for 40 minutes, until the top is lightly golden and the filling is cooked but still soft to the touch.

Immediately slide the flamiche on to a wire rack, using a large palette knife. Gently lift the flan ring off. Serve the quiche warm or tepid, but not piping hot.

Prune tartlets

SERVES 6

480g (1lb 1oz) flan pastry
(see page 180)

30g (2 tbsp) butter, to grease

flour, to dust

For the filling

²/₃ quantity (500g/1lb 2oz) crème
pâtissière (see page 206), freshly
made, replacing half the flour with
custard powder

24 very moist prunes, preferably
Agen, stoned

These rustic tartlets remind me of my childhood, when
they were on show in every pâtisserie and bakery window.
Serve as a dessert, or at teatime.

Grease 6 tartlet tins, 10 cm (4in) in diameter (3 cm/1¼in deep), and
place in the fridge. Roll out the pastry into a rectangle 2–3 mm
(⅛in) thick. Put the tartlet tins on the work surface, then lightly roll
the pastry round the rolling pin, and carefully unroll it over the tins.
Use your thumb and index finger to push the pastry into the tins to
line them. Press the rolling pin on to the tins to cut off the excess
pastry, then lightly crimp the edges. Leave the tartlets to rest in the
fridge for at least 20 minutes. Preheat the oven to 200°C/400°F/
Gas 6.

Prick the bottom of the pastry cases in 3 or 4 places with a fork. Line
the bases with greaseproof paper and fill the tins to the top with
baking beans or dried pulses. Bake blind for 12 minutes, until three-
quarters cooked. Remove the beans and paper and leave the cases
to cool. Increase the oven temperature to 220°C/425°F/Gas 7.

Divide the hot crème pâtissière between the tartlet cases. Put
4 prunes into each one, pressing them down so that they are two-
thirds immersed in the cream. Bake for 5–6 minutes until the tops
are lightly browned. Unmould the tartlets with the aid of a small
knife tip and cool on a wire rack. Serve warm or just cold.

Lemon tart

Serves 8–10

550g (1lb 4oz) pâte sucrée
(see page 181)

20g (1½ tbsp) butter, to grease

flour, to dust

2–3 tbsp brown sugar, to glaze

For the filling

finely grated zest and juice of
4 lemons

9 medium eggs

375g (scant 2 cups) caster
(superfine) sugar

300ml (1¼ cups) double (heavy)
cream, chilled

eggwash (1 egg yolk beaten with
½ tsp milk)

*Buy unwaxed lemons and wash
and dry well before grating the
zest. When you have squeezed all
the juice from the lemons, strain it
through a fine chinois to eliminate
the pulp and pips.*

The amazing freshness of my lemon tart makes it a firm
favourite and it has become a classic recipe. If preferred,
top the filling with meringue (see page 243) rather than
glaze with sugar.

For the tart case, grease a 20cm (8in) flan ring (4cm/1½in deep)
and place on a baking sheet in the fridge. Roll out the pastry into
a round 3–4mm (⅛in) thick and use to line the flan ring (see
page 182). Rest in the fridge for 20 minutes. Preheat the oven
to 200°C/400°F/Gas 6.

For the filling, combine the lemon zest and juice in a bowl. Lightly
whisk the eggs with the sugar in another bowl. Whip the cream to
a light ribbon consistency. Mix the eggs into the lemon juice, then
fold this mixture into the cream. Cover and refrigerate.

Prick the bottom of the pastry case, line with greaseproof paper and
baking beans or dried pulses and bake blind for 20 minutes. Remove
the beans and paper and leave to cool for 1–2 minutes. Brush the
inside of the pastry case with eggwash and return to the oven for
5 minutes. Reduce the oven temperature to 150°C/300°F/Gas 2.

Give the filling a light stir, then pour it into the pastry case and bake
for about 1 hour 20 minutes. Cut off any excess pastry from the rim
with a small knife. Leave the tart on the baking sheet for about 20
minutes, then lift off the flan ring. Using a large palette knife, slide
the tart on to a wire rack and leave to cool for 3–4 hours.

Finish the tart shortly before serving. Sprinkle the brown sugar
evenly over the surface, then brown it with a cook's blowtorch or
under a very hot grill (broiler), as you would a crème brûlée. Cut the
tart into slices, using a long, thin, sharp-bladed knife.

Strawberry tart

SERVES 8

400g (14oz) pâte sucrée (see page 181)

20g (1½ tbsp) butter, to grease

flour, to dust

75ml (5 tbsp) double (heavy) cream

30g (2½ tbsp) sugar

150g (5½oz) crème pâtissière (see page 206), cooled

500g (1lb 2oz) strawberries, hulled

icing (confectioners') sugar, to dust

red berry coulis (see page 158) (optional)

I like to serve this delectable tart with a little red fruit coulis on the side – the perfect complement.

For the pastry case, grease a 20cm (8in) flan ring (3cm/1¼in deep), and place on a baking sheet in the fridge. Roll out the pastry into a round 3–4mm (⅛in) thick and use to line the flan ring (see page 182). Leave to rest in the fridge for at least 20 minutes. Preheat the oven to 200°C/400°F/Gas 6.

Prick the bottom of the pastry case, line with greaseproof paper and baking beans or dried pulses and bake blind for 20 minutes. Remove the beans and paper and return to the oven for another 10 minutes. Slide the cooked pastry case on to a wire rack and carefully lift off the flan ring. Leave to cool.

For the filling, whip the cream with the sugar to a ribbon consistency, then add the crème pâtissière and mix thoroughly with a whisk. Spread evenly over the bottom of the pastry case. Halve or quarter larger strawberries, leaving small ones whole. Arrange on top of the creamy filling. Dust with icing sugar just before serving.

Cut the delicate tart into slices, using a long, thin, sharp-bladed knife. Serve with a little fruit coulis if you like.

Pasta dough

Makes about 350g (12oz)

250g (1¾ cups) Italian '00' flour

1 medium egg

4 medium egg yolks

1 tbsp olive oil

pinch of salt

Fresh pasta will keep well-wrapped in the fridge for a day or two, but it is best cooked as soon as it is cut.

Put the flour in a mound on a clean surface (preferably marble) and make a well in the middle. Put the whole egg, egg yolks, 1tbsp cold water, the olive oil and salt into the well.

Using your fingertips, mix all the ingredients in the well together, then gradually draw the flour into the centre, little by little.

When the dough is almost completely amalgamated, knead it 4 or 5 times with the heel of your hand, then roll it into a ball, wrap in cling film (plastic wrap), and refrigerate for 1 hour.

Divide the pasta dough in half; re-wrap one portion. Roll the other portion through a pasta machine, starting on the widest setting. Continue to roll it through the machine repeatedly, narrowing the setting by one notch each time until the sheet of dough is 1.5mm (½₀in) thick. Roll it through once more to prevent shrinkage when you cut it.

continued overleaf

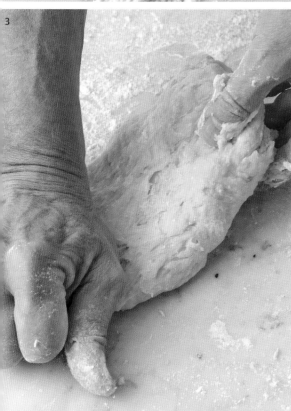

Fit the appropriate cutter on the machine and cut the dough into linguine, spaghetti or tagliatelle.

Lay the strands on a sheet of greaseproof paper or lightly floured parchment to aerate them and prevent tangling.

To cook the pasta, bring a large pan of lightly salted water to the boil with a few drops of olive oil added. Add the freshly cut pasta and cook for about 1½– 2 minutes, until it is al dente (tender, but firm to the bite). The precise cooking time is determined by the width and thickness of the pasta strands.

Pasta serving suggestions

Tagliatelle with young spring vegetables All the following vegetables can be used to enhance fresh pasta: peas, broccoli florets, broad (fava) beans, sliced courgettes (zucchini), mangetout (snow peas). Simply blanch them for a few seconds and refresh, then sweat gently in a little olive oil for a minute or two. Add some snipped basil leaves and a touch of crushed garlic before tossing the vegetables with freshly cooked tagliatelle. Serve a bowl of freshly grated Parmesan on the side to complement the wonderful flavours.

Spaghetti with seafood and cherry tomatoes Steamed and shelled mussels, peeled prawns (shrimp) and sliced, lightly poached or pan-fried scallops, are exquisite mixed into freshly cooked spaghetti. I like to add some roasted cherry tomatoes (prepared in advance, as for Portuguese-style scrambled egg, see page 96), and to serve a bowl of pesto on the side (see below).

Linguine with pesto Pesto is the perfect partner for freshly made pasta. You can buy this ready made, but it's so easy to prepare, tastes far superior if it's freshly made, and the aromas will perfume your house. Simply pound 4 crushed garlic cloves with 20 basil leaves and 30g (1oz) toasted pine nuts, using a pestle and mortar, then add 100g (3½oz) freshly grated Parmesan. Slowly trickle in 150ml (scant ⅔ cup) olive oil, stirring continuously with the pestle. Once the pesto is smooth, season to taste with salt and pepper. Toss freshly cooked linguine with pesto and serve with extra grated Parmesan.

Linguine alla carbonara

SERVES 4

3 tbsp olive oil

200g (7oz) onions, chopped

1 garlic clove, finely chopped

200g (7oz) thin slices of pancetta or bacon

150ml (scant ²/₃ cup) double (heavy) cream

4 egg yolks

10g (⅓oz) snipped flat parsley leaves

salt and freshly ground pepper

350g (12oz) linguine, preferably fresh (see pages 194–6)

60g (2oz) Parmesan, freshly grated

A successful carbonara depends on good pasta cooked to perfection at the last moment, a very hot serving dish and the rapid mixing in of cream and egg to create a glistening sauce, which lightly coats the pasta.

Warm a deep serving dish in the oven at 170°C/325°F/Gas 3 for 10 minutes.

Heat 1 tbsp olive oil in a non-stick frying pan over a very low heat, add the onions and sweat gently for 2 minutes. Add the garlic, stir well and transfer to a bowl.

In the cleaned, dried frying pan, lightly brown the pancetta or bacon slices over a medium heat. Tip on to a board and cut into 1cm (½in) pieces, then add to the onions and keep warm.

In a bowl, mix the cream, egg yolks and parsley together, and season lightly with salt and pepper.

Bring a large saucepan of salted water to the boil and add 1 tbsp olive oil. Add the linguine and cook for 1–2 minutes, until al dente, or done to your liking, then drain.

Immediately take the serving dish from oven, add the remaining 1 tbsp olive oil and put in the pasta. Quickly pour on the cream mixture, mix rapidly with tongs, then add the bacon and onion mixture. Sprinkle with Parmesan, mix well but not too thoroughly, and serve immediately.

Custard, Creams & Mousses

With their different textures, some creams and mousses are used as fillings or toppings for desserts and cakes, while others, like my rich chocolate & orange mousse (see page 216) and little cream caramel & coffee pots (see page 211), are stand-alone desserts. They all have something in common, though. They are light, creamy and rather rich, so they should be served in small portions. Most can be prepared in advance and kept in the fridge for a day or two. Of course, crème anglaise (see page 202) is the perfect accompaniment for many desserts; I also love it with summer berries like wild strawberries, blueberries and raspberries. I'm also partial to freshly cooked waffles topped with Chiboust cream (see page 207). Crème brûlée has long been a favourite of dessert lovers and I urge you to try my favourite, pistachio crème brûlée (see page 212).

Crème anglaise

MAKES ABOUT 750ML (3 CUPS)
(6–8 SERVINGS)

500ml (2 cups) milk

125g (scant ²/₃ cup) caster (superfine) sugar

1 vanilla pod, split lengthways

6 egg yolks

Put the milk in a saucepan with two-thirds of the sugar, add the vanilla pod and bring to the boil over a medium heat.

Meanwhile, whisk the egg yolks and remaining sugar together in a bowl to a light ribbon consistency.

Pour the boiling milk on to the egg yolks, whisking continuously, then pour the mixture back into the saucepan.

Cook over a low heat, stirring with a wooden spatula or spoon, until the custard lightly coats the back of the spatula. When you run your finger through, it should leave a clear trace. Immediately take the pan off the heat.

Unless you are serving the crème anglaise warm, pour into a bowl and leave to cool, stirring occasionally to prevent a skin forming. When cold, pass through a chinois.

The custard will keep in a covered container in the fridge for up to 3 days.

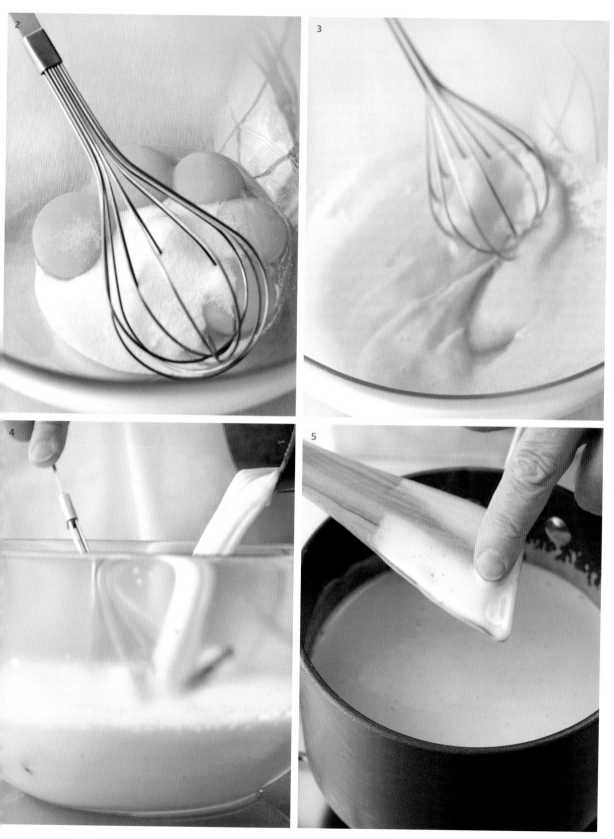

Minted crème anglaise

MAKES ABOUT 750 ML (3 CUPS)
(6 – 8 SERVINGS)

500ml (2 cups) milk

125g (scant ²/₃ cup) caster (superfine) sugar

75g (2½oz) mint leaves and stalks, coarsely chopped

6 egg yolks

The freshness of this mint-flavoured custard goes brilliantly with all berries. It is also excellent with chocolate ice cream (see page 228) or my chocolate truffle cake with candied kumquats (see page 259).

Put the milk in a saucepan with two-thirds of the sugar and bring to the boil over a medium heat. Add the mint, take the pan off the heat, cover and leave to infuse for 10 minutes.

In a bowl, whisk the egg yolks and the remaining sugar to a light ribbon consistency. Bring the milk just back to the boil, then pour on to the egg yolks, whisking continuously. Pour the mixture back into the saucepan. Cook over a low heat, stirring all the time with a wooden spatula or spoon, until the custard lightly coats the back of the spatula (see page 202).

Immediately pass the crème anglaise through a chinois into a bowl and set aside until completely cold, stirring occasionally with a spatula to prevent a skin forming. Once cold, cover with cling film (plastic wrap) and keep in the fridge for up to 3 days until ready to use.

Crème pâtissière

Makes about 750g (3 cups)

6 egg yolks

125g (scant ⅔ cup) caster
(superfine) sugar

40g (heaped ¼ cup) plain
(all-purpose) flour

500ml (2 cups) milk

1 vanilla pod, split lengthways

a little icing (confectioners') sugar
or butter

*For a lighter textured crème
pâtissiere, I fold in 20–50% whipped
cream (ie 150–300ml/scant ⅔–1¼
cups). Or for a rich velvety texture, I
incorporate 10% whipped softened
butter (ie 75g/5 tbsp).*

Crème pâtissière – or pastry cream – has many roles in
pâtisserie, including fillings for choux buns and sweet tarts,
and my Chiboust cream.

Combine the egg yolks and one-third of the sugar in a bowl and
whisk to a light ribbon consistency. Add the flour and whisk it in
thoroughly.

In a saucepan, heat the milk with the rest of the sugar and the
vanilla pod. As soon as it comes to the boil, pour it on to the egg
yolk mixture, stirring as you go. Mix well, then return the mixture
to the saucepan.

Bring to the boil over a medium heat, stirring continuously with the
whisk. Allow the mixture to bubble, still stirring, for 2 minutes, then
tip it into a bowl.

To prevent a skin forming, dust the surface with a veil of icing sugar
or dot all over with little flakes of butter. Once cold, the pastry
cream can be kept in the fridge for up to 3 days. Remove the vanilla
pod before using.

Chiboust cream

MAKES ABOUT 1.2KG (2LB 10OZ)

6 egg yolks

80g (6½ tbsp) sugar

30g (⅓ cup) custard powder

350ml (1½ cups) milk

1 vanilla pod, split lengthways

a little icing (confectioners') sugar, to dust

1 quantity Italian meringue (see page 240)

This wonderfully rich, velvety cream is perfect for serving with waffles, filling crêpes and topping fruit tarts to make them even more tempting.

For the pastry cream, combine the egg yolks and one-third of the sugar in a bowl and whisk to a light ribbon consistency. Add the custard powder and whisk thoroughly. Heat the milk with the rest of the sugar and the vanilla pod. As soon as it comes to the boil, pour it on to the egg yolk mixture, stirring all the time.

Return the mixture to the pan and bring to the boil over a medium heat, stirring with the whisk. Allow to bubble, still stirring, for 2 minutes, then tip it into a bowl. Dust the surface with icing sugar to prevent a skin forming.

Make the Italian meringue (following the step-by-step instructions on page 240).

Remove the vanilla pod from the pastry cream. Using a whisk, stir in one-third of the Italian meringue, then delicately fold in the rest using a spatula to make a smooth cream. Use the Chiboust cream straightaway, or see note (below).

For a firmer consistency, or to keep the cream for a few hours after making it, soak 2 sheets of leaf gelatine in cold water for a few minutes, then drain well and fold them into the hot pastry cream as soon as you have made it, stirring until melted.

Blackberry ripple

SERVES 6

350g (12oz) blackberries, plus extra to serve (optional)

130g (²/₃ cup) caster (superfine) sugar

juice of 1 lemon

100ml (scant 1 cup) double (heavy) cream

⅓ quantity (250g/9oz) crème pâtissière (see page 206), cooled

2 egg whites

You may need to adjust the quantity of sugar for cooking the blackberries according to how ripe they are. This mousse is equally delicious made with flavourful strawberries or raspberries.

Put the blackberries in a saucepan with 100g (½ cup) sugar and heat very gently, stirring with a wooden spoon from time to time. When the mixture comes to a simmer, cook gently for another 10 minutes. Transfer to a blender or food processor and whiz to a purée, then strain through a muslin-lined chinois into a bowl. Leave this coulis to cool, stirring occasionally to prevent a skin forming. When cold, stir in the lemon juice.

Whip the cream to a ribbon consistency, then fold into the cooled crème pâtissière.

Whisk the egg whites in a clean bowl to a thick foam, then add the remaining sugar and whisk to soft peaks. Gently fold in the pastry cream mixture, without overworking.

Very delicately mix in the cold blackberry coulis to create a ripple effect. Divide the mousse between 6 glass dishes and refrigerate for 2–3 hours before serving.

Serve the mousse on its own, or with extra berries.

Little cream caramel & coffee pots

SERVES 6

180g (scant 1 cup) caster (superfine) sugar

250ml (1 cup) milk

100ml (scant ½ cup) double (heavy) cream

15g (1½ tbsp) instant coffee granules or powder

3 eggs

2 egg yolks

40g (3¼ tbsp) soft brown sugar, to caramelise (optional)

Soft as velvet, creamy, satisfyingly long in the mouth and full of flavour – I can happily eat two of these unctuous creams...

Have ready 6 little ovenproof pots, about 5cm (2in) in diameter and 6cm (2½in) deep.

Put 100g (½ cup) caster sugar in a small heavy-based pan and melt over a medium heat, stirring with a wooden spoon until it is liquid and turns a pale caramel colour. Immediately pour into the pots and rotate them to coat the insides with the hot caramel, using a cloth to protect your hands. Leave to cool completely. Preheat the oven to 120°C/250°F/Gas ½.

Combine the milk, cream, coffee and 50g (¼ cup) sugar in a saucepan and gently bring to the boil, stirring to dissolve the coffee. Whisk the eggs, yolks and remaining sugar in a bowl for 1 minute. Pour the boiling milk on to the egg mixture, whisking as you go.

Divide the mixture between the caramel-lined pots. Stand them in a deep ovenproof dish lined with greaseproof paper and pour in hot (not boiling) water to come about halfway up the sides. Cook in the oven for 45 minutes, or until a thin-bladed knife tip inserted into the centre of a custard comes out clean. If necessary, cook for an extra 5–10 minutes. Place the pots on a wire rack to cool, then refrigerate for several hours.

I like to caramelise the creams before serving. To do this, sprinkle the tops with the brown sugar and caramelise with a cook's blowtorch for a few seconds. If you prefer, simply unmould the creams on to plates – the caramel will run out as you do so.

Pistachio crème brûlée

500ml (2 cups) milk

500ml (2 cups) whipping cream

60g (2oz) pistachio paste

150g (¾ cup) caster (superfine) sugar

200g (7oz) egg yolks (about 10)

70g (6 tbsp) demerara sugar

If you can't find pistachio paste, you can make your own by pounding freshly skinned pistachios in a mortar to make a smooth paste.

Preheat the oven to 120°C/250°F/Gas ½. To make the custard, heat the milk, cream, pistachio paste and 90g (scant ½ cup) caster sugar in a saucepan, whisking until well blended, then slowly bring to the boil.

Meanwhile, in a bowl, lightly whisk the egg yolks with the remaining caster sugar. As soon as the milk mixture comes to the boil, gradually pour it on to the egg mixture, whisking all the time.

Ladle the custard into 15cm (6in) gratin dishes and place on a baking tray. Cook in the oven for 30 minutes, or until just set. Transfer the dishes to a wire rack and leave until the custards are cold, then chill until ready to serve.

Just before serving, sprinkle the tops with the demerara sugar and caramelise with a cook's blowtorch, or under a very hot grill (broiler), to make a thin, pale nut-brown topping. Serve immediately.

Rich chocolate and orange mousse

150g (5½oz) plain (bittersweet) chocolate (55–70% cocoa solids), chopped into small pieces

1 tbsp liquid glucose

2 egg yolks

150ml (scant ⅔ cup) double (heavy) cream

30g (¼ cup) icing (confectioners') sugar

To decorate

1 orange, washed

100g (½ cup) caster (superfine) sugar

Fresh orange segments and toasted brioche complement this rich mousse perfectly.

First prepare the decoration. Finely pare the zest from the orange into fine strips, using a zester. Place in a saucepan, cover with cold water and bring to the boil over a medium heat. Refresh and drain, then repeat this process twice more. Put the zests in a small pan with 100ml (scant ½ cup) water and the sugar. Bring to the boil and bubble for 1 minute, then leave the zests to cool in the syrup. When cold, drain and set aside.

To make the chocolate mousse, place the chocolate in a bowl set over a pan of gently simmering water to melt (making sure the bowl isn't in direct contact with the water). When the chocolate has melted, take the bowl off the heat. Mix the glucose with the egg yolks and 2 tbsp warm water, then mix into the melted chocolate.

In another bowl, whip the cream with the icing sugar to a ribbon consistency, then delicately fold into the mousse mixture, without overworking it.

Pour one-third of the mousse mixture into 4 glasses or glass dishes, about 6cm (2½in) in diameter, or 4 large ramekins. Scatter one-third of the zests on top. Repeat these layers twice, finishing with a layer of mousse sprinkled with orange zest. Refrigerate for an hour before serving. If chilled for longer, remove 30 minutes before serving.

illustrated on previous page

Caramel mousse

SERVES 8–10

For the caramel cream

400 ml (1¾ cups) whipping cream

150 ml (scant ⅔ cup) liquid glucose

200 g (1 cup) caster (superfine) sugar

50 g (3½ tbsp) butter, diced

For the pâte à bombe

60 g (⅓ cup) caster (superfine) sugar

30 g (2 tbsp) liquid glucose

6 egg yolks

3 sheets of leaf gelatine, soaked in cold water

220 ml (scant 1 cup) whipping cream

Serve this rich, creamy mousse in lightly chilled glasses, but don't chill the mousse before serving. Thin slices of Genoese sponge (see page 252) make an excellent accompaniment.

To make the caramel cream, heat the cream and glucose in a saucepan until boiling. Meanwhile, put the sugar in a small heavy-based pan and melt it gently, stirring with a wooden spoon until it turns pale golden. Take the pan off the heat, immediately pour on the cream mixture, then return to a low heat and gently bring back to the boil. Bubble for 2 minutes, then turn off the heat and whisk in the butter. Pass the caramel cream through a chinois and leave to cool (to about 24°C/75°F).

For the pâte à bombe, put 80 ml (⅓ cup) water, the sugar and glucose in a heavy-based pan and dissolve over a low heat, brushing the sugar crystals down the side of the pan with a pastry brush dipped in cold water. Let the syrup bubble for 2–3 minutes until it turns light caramel at the edge. Put the egg yolks in a bowl and pour on the syrup in a thin stream, whisking constantly. Stand the bowl over a pan of boiling water and whisk the mixture for about 5 minutes, until it reaches 70°C/150°F. Take the bowl off the pan and carry on whisking until the temperature has reduced to about 24°C/75°F. Squeeze excess water from the gelatine then dissolve in 2 tbsp hot water and fold into the bombe mixture.

In another bowl, whip the cream to a ribbon consistency. When the caramel cream and the bombe mixture are both about the same temperature, delicately fold them together with the whisk, then fold in the whipped cream. The mousse is now ready to serve.

Chilled lemon soufflé

1 tbsp groundnut oil

6 medium eggs, separated

130g (²/₃ cup) caster (superfine) sugar

finely grated zest and juice of 4 lemons

2 sheets of leaf gelatine, soaked in cold water

500ml (2 cups) double (heavy) cream

To decorate

2 lemons, washed

200g (1 cup) sugar

20g (2 tbsp) flaked (sliced) almonds, lightly toasted

This is equally delicious served chilled or iced – the choice is yours.

First prepare a soufflé dish, 13cm (5in) in diameter and 8cm (3¼in) high. Wrap a triple thick band of greaseproof paper around the dish, wide enough to extend 6–8cm (2½–3¼in) above the rim. Secure with tape and string. Brush the exposed inside paper with oil. Place in the fridge.

Whisk the egg yolks, 80g (6½ tbsp) sugar and the lemon zest together in a bowl until the mixture is thick enough to leave a light trail when you lift the whisk. Warm the lemon juice, squeeze out excess water from the gelatine leaves, then dissolve them in the lemon juice. Whisk into the egg yolk mixture and continue to whisk for 1 minute. In another bowl, whip the cream to a ribbon consistency, then fold into the lemon mixture.

Whisk the egg whites to a thick foam, then whisk in the remaining 50g (¼ cup) sugar to soft peaks. Fold into the soufflé mixture and immediately spoon it into the dish to come 4–5cm (1½–2in) above the rim. Gently smooth the surface with the back of a spoon. Put the soufflé in the fridge for at least 6–8 hours, or freeze for 3–4 hours before serving.

For the decoration, slice the lemons into thin rounds, halve the slices and place in a saucepan with 200ml (scant 1 cup) water and the sugar. Bring to the boil and bubble gently for 2 minutes. Leave to cool; keep the lemon slices in the syrup until ready to use.

To serve, remove the paper collar from the soufflé. Sprinkle the almonds over the centre and arrange the lemon slices around them. Serve immediately.

Lemon curd

MAKES 550G (1LB 4OZ)

200g (scant 1 cup) butter, diced

200g (1 cup) caster (superfine) sugar

grated zest and juice of 3 lemons

4 egg yolks

Although we think of a fruit curd as a preserve, it is more like a rich custard, in which the fruit juice effectively takes the place of milk, and butter adds richness. I use this lemon curd to fill tiny pâte sucrée tartlets (see page 181), and serve them as petits fours.

Put the butter, sugar and lemon zest and juice into a heatproof bowl. Stand the bowl over a saucepan of simmering water (making sure the base of the bowl isn't in direct contact with the water). The butter will begin to melt after a few minutes. Whisk the mixture until it is completely smooth.

Add the egg yolks and whisk vigorously for about 10 minutes, until the mixture begins to thicken. Pour the lemon curd into a jar or small ramekins, cover with cling film (plastic wrap), and leave in the fridge.

Serve this divinely rich lemon curd straight from the jar or ramekins. Spread it like butter on toasted brioche or scones for a real treat.

For orange curd, substitute the lemons with 2 oranges and boil the juice to reduce by one-third before you start. I adore orange curd spread on crêpes (see page 154).

Ice Creams

Based on eggs, milk, sugar and a little cream, homemade ice cream is quick and easy to make, and tastes infinitely better than any bought variety. Ice creams originated in China and were introduced into Europe by the Italians in the 17th century. Their popularity soon spread. An ice cream maker is a good investment, especially if you have children. Made with fresh ingredients, without artificial colourings or preservatives, homemade ice cream is much healthier than its commercial equivalent. To enjoy the ice cream at its best, eat it soon after churning. Ice creams can be served alone or with meringues, biscuits or petits fours. Red berry coulis is delicious poured over vanilla ice cream, as is chocolate sauce on banana ice cream. And do try my Camembert ice cream (see page 234). Served with digestive biscuits, it's a delight.

Vanilla ice cream

SERVES 8

1 quantity crème anglaise (see page 202)

100ml (scant ½ cup) double (heavy) cream (optional)

The texture of ice cream is best if it is served shortly after churning.

Adding double cream makes this classic ice cream extra rich and creamy, but you can make it without.

When the crème anglaise is ready, pour it into a stainless steel or glass bowl. Stand the base of the bowl on ice to hasten the cooling, and stir with a spatula from time to time to prevent a skin forming. When it is cold, remove the vanilla pod, then pour into an ice cream maker and start churning.

After about 10 minutes, the ice cream should be half-frozen. If you are using the cream, add it in a steady stream while the machine is still running.

Carry on churning for 10–15 minutes, until the ice cream has set. It should be firm but still creamy.

Transfer the ice cream to a chilled freezerproof container and keep it in the freezer until ready to serve.

Cinnamon ice cream

SERVES 8

1 quantity crème anglaise (see page 202), infused with a 20g (²/₃ oz) cinnamon stick, lightly broken, instead of vanilla

100ml (scant ½ cup) double (heavy) cream (optional)

To serve (optional)

8 Cox's or Bramley apples

caster (superfine) sugar, to sprinkle

8 knobs of butter

Everyone adores this wonderful ice cream when they taste it. I find it goes particularly well with baked apples.

Make the ice cream following the method on page 224, leaving the cinnamon in the mixture until you are ready to churn it. Strain the infused mixture through a fine chinois or muslin into the ice cream maker and churn until the ice cream is the correct consistency.

If serving the ice cream with baked apples, use an apple corer to remove the cores, then make an incision with a knife tip all round the circumference of each apple. Stand them in a deep ovenproof dish, sprinkle with a little sugar and put a knob of butter on each apple. Pour a little water into the dish and bake at 180°C/350°F/ Gas 4 for 40 minutes. Leave to cool slightly.

Once the apples are just warm, put them on individual plates, top them with a large scoop of cinnamon ice cream and serve.

Chocolate ice cream

SERVES 6

150ml (scant ⅔ cup) milk

150ml (scant ⅔ cup) double (heavy) cream

80g (6½ tbsp) caster (superfine) sugar

3 egg yolks

100g (3½oz) plain (bittersweet) chocolate (55–70% cocoa solids), cut into small pieces

I like to serve this ice cream scooped into coffee meringue shells (see page 244) but, of course, it will complement many desserts and is delicious served on its own.

Put the milk and cream in a saucepan with two-thirds of the sugar and bring to the boil over a medium heat. Meanwhile, whisk the egg yolks and the remaining sugar together in a bowl to a light ribbon consistency. Pour the boiling milk on to the egg yolks, whisking continuously, then pour the mixture back into the saucepan.

Cook over a low heat, stirring with a wooden spatula or spoon, until the custard lightly coats the back of the spatula. When you run your finger through, it should leave a clear trace (see page 203). Immediately take the pan off the heat, add the pieces of chocolate and stir with a whisk until melted.

Pour the mixture into a bowl and leave to cool over ice, stirring occasionally to prevent a skin forming. When it is cold, pass through a chinois into the ice cream maker, then churn it for 20–25 minutes, following the method on page 224, until the ice cream is firm but still creamy.

Tea ice cream

SERVES 8

1 quantity crème anglaise (see page 202), infused with 50g (1¾oz) loose-leaf Earl Grey or jasmine tea, instead of vanilla (see note)

100ml (scant ⅔ cup) double (heavy) cream (optional)

For optimum flavour, add the tea leaves to the milk just before it reaches the boil.

The only teas I use for making ice cream are Earl Grey and jasmine, but you might like to experiment with other flavours. I like to serve this ice cream with my raspberry macarons (see page 250).

Make the ice cream following the method on page 224, leaving the tea leaves in the mixture until you churn it. Strain the infused mixture through a chinois or muslin into the ice cream maker and churn until the ice cream is the correct consistency.

Serve scooped into individual dishes, with dessert biscuits or petit fours, such as raspberry macarons.

Stem ginger ice cream

SERVES 8

1 quantity crème anglaise (see page 202), made without vanilla

75g (2½oz) preserved stem ginger in syrup, drained and chopped

30g (heaped ⅓ cup) desiccated (dried shredded) coconut

I like to serve this ice cream on small plates with wafer-thin slices of fresh pineapple.

Even those who don't like ginger will be tempted by this ice cream. It's amazing how ice cream can elevate ingredients to a different level.

Pour the hot crème anglaise into a food processor, add the chopped ginger and whiz for 1 minute, then strain through a chinois into a bowl. Stand the base of the bowl on ice to hasten the cooling, and stir with a spatula from time to time to prevent a skin forming on the surface.

Mix in the desiccated coconut, then pour the mixture into the ice cream maker. Churn for 20–25 minutes, following the method on page 224, until the ice cream is firm but still creamy. Serve scooped into dishes or on to small plates.

Camembert ice cream

SERVES 8

500ml (2 cups) milk

6 egg yolks

25g (2 tbsp) caster (superfine) sugar

pinch of salt

1 fine ripe Camembert, about 300g (10½oz)

small pinch of cayenne

8 drops of Tabasco

I first created this original ice cream in the 1960s. I like to serve it as a palate-cleanser, accompanied by small radishes, a few tender celery leaves and some biscuits for cheese.

Bring the milk to the boil in a saucepan. Meanwhile, in a bowl, whisk the egg yolks with the sugar and salt to a light ribbon consistency. Pour the boiling milk on to the egg yolks, whisking continuously, then pour the mixture back into the saucepan.

Cook over a low heat, stirring with a wooden spatula, until the custard lightly coats the back of the spatula. When you run your finger through, it should leave a clear trace (see page 203). Immediately take the pan off the heat and pour the custard into a bowl.

Cut off the minimum of crust from the Camembert, then cut the cheese into thin slivers over the custard. Mix well with a whisk until the cheese has melted, then add the cayenne and Tabasco.

Stand the base of the bowl on ice to hasten the cooling, and stir with a spatula from time to time to prevent a skin forming. Pour the mixture into an ice cream maker and churn for 20–25 minutes, following the method on page 224, until the ice cream is firm but still creamy. Serve in individual bowls.

Illustrated on page 223

Chestnut ice cream

Serves 8

500ml (2 cups) milk

150g (5½oz) sweetened chestnut purée

100g (½ cup) caster (superfine) sugar

6 egg yolks

2 tbsp rum (optional)

100ml (scant ½ cup) double (heavy) cream

100g (3½oz) marrons glacés or marrons in syrup (optional)

This is one of my favourite ice creams. I sometimes serve it with a jug of simple chocolate sauce – just warm melted plain chocolate with a dash of milk added.

Put the milk, chestnut purée and two-thirds of the sugar in a saucepan and bring to the boil over a medium heat. Meanwhile, whisk the egg yolks and the remaining sugar together in a bowl to a light ribbon consistency. Pour the boiling milk on to the egg yolks, whisking continuously, then pour the mixture back into the saucepan.

Cook over a low heat, stirring with a wooden spatula or spoon, until the custard lightly coats the back of the spatula. When you run your finger through, it should leave a clear trace (see page 203). Immediately take the pan off the heat and pour into a bowl. Add the rum if desired and leave to cool over ice, stirring occasionally to prevent a skin forming.

When cold, pass the mixture through a chinois into the ice cream maker and churn for 20–25 minutes following the method on page 224 and adding the cream as directed. The ice cream is ready when it is firm but still creamy.

Serve scoops of ice cream piled into shallow bowls and topped with small pieces of marrons glacés if you like.

Banana & sultana ice cream

SERVES 8

30g (2 tbsp) butter

50g (¼ cup) caster (superfine) sugar

1 ripe banana, about 180g (6¼oz), sliced

juice of 1 lemon

1 quantity crème anglaise (see page 202), made with 25g (1½ tbsp) sugar and without vanilla

60g (scant ½ cup) sultanas (golden raisins)

This ice cream is superb served with warm banana halves, quickly sautéed in butter and drizzled with a ribbon of apricot glaze.

Heat the butter in a frying pan, add the sugar, then the banana slices and cook over a medium heat for 1–2 minutes, until the banana is lightly caramelised. Pour on the lemon juice, then mix the banana into the hot crème anglaise, stirring with a spatula.

Transfer the mixture to a blender and whiz for 1 minute, then pass through a chinois into a bowl. Stand over ice to hasten the cooling, and stir with a spatula from time to time to prevent a skin forming. Meanwhile, blanch the sultanas in boiling water for 1 minute, then remove and refresh in cold water, drain and set aside.

Pour the banana mixture into an ice cream maker and churn for 20–25 minutes, following the method on page 224, until the ice cream is firm but still creamy. Stir in the sultanas a minute or two before removing the ice cream from the machine.

Scoop the ice cream into dishes and serve with caramelised banana halves if you like.

Meringues
& Sponges

Meringues are crunchy, sponges are soft and mellow, but both are light and delicious. They form the basis of many desserts and go well with ice creams, coulis, creams and mousses. French meringues are very quick and easy to make – all you need is some egg whites and a little sugar – and they freeze well. The phenomenon of whisking egg whites into snowy peaks is intriguing. Whisking traps air bubbles inside the whites, which inflate to 6 to 8 times their original volume. Pavlova (see page 247) is one of my favourite meringue desserts. Versatile Genoese sponge takes only 20 minutes to make and can be kept wrapped in cling film for up to 3 days in the fridge, or frozen. Eat it plain with fruit salad, ice cream or jam, or on its own. Genoese is also the base for my chocolate truffle cake (see page 259) and raspberry roulade (see page 256).

Italian meringue

MAKES ABOUT 600G (1LB 5OZ)

360g (heaped 1¾ cups) caster (superfine) sugar

30g (2 tbsp) liquid glucose (optional)

6 medium egg whites

A sugar thermometer is essential for preparing this meringue. The liquid glucose prevents crystals from forming in the egg whites when the sugar syrup is added.

Pour 80ml (⅓ cup) water into a heavy-based saucepan, add the sugar and glucose if using, and set over a medium heat. Bring to the boil, stirring occasionally and brushing down any crystals that form on the side of the pan, using a pastry brush moistened with water. Increase the heat and place a sugar thermometer in the boiling syrup to register when it reaches 110°C/230°F.

Still keeping an eye on the syrup, beat the egg whites until they hold peaks, either by hand or with an electric mixer. Stop cooking the syrup the moment it reaches 121°C/250°F. Take the pan off the heat and let the bubbling subside for 30 seconds. Pour the syrup on to the beaten egg whites in a thin, steady stream, whisking at low speed with the mixer or by hand until very firm.

When all the syrup has been absorbed, continue to beat at low speed for 15 minutes, until the meringue is almost completely cold (30–35°C/86–95°F). It is now ready to use (see overleaf).

The meringue can be kept in an airtight container in the fridge for up to 48 hours before use.

Uses for Italian meringue

Lemon meringue tart Follow the recipe for my classic lemon tart (see page 190), omitting the brown sugar glaze. Instead, pipe one-third of a quantity (250g/9oz) of Italian meringue (see page 240) over the top of the tart to cover the filling, using a piping bag fitted with a fluted nozzle. Wave a cook's blowtorch over the surface until the meringue is lightly tinged browned, or place under a very hot grill (broiler) for a few seconds.

Baked Alaska Line a soufflé dish or heatproof salad bowl with food-safe cling film (plastic wrap) and layer two different ice creams, such as chocolate (see page 228) and vanilla (see page 224) in the dish. Place in the freezer for several hours to harden. Make a Genoese sponge (see page 252) 4–5cm (1½–2in) wider than the base of the dish. Using a serrated knife, slice off the top 1–2cm (½–¾in) of the sponge to make a flat base for the baked Alaska.

Dip the base of the dish into hot water for about 20 seconds, then unmould the ice cream and invert it on to the sponge base. Using a piping bag fitted with a large fluted nozzle, pipe half a quantity of Italian meringue (see page 240) all over the ice cream to cover it completely. Place under a hot grill (broiler) for a few seconds to lightly brown the meringue, or do this with a cook's blowtorch.

Buttercream Measure an equal weight of butter to Italian meringue, cut it into small pieces and soften at room temperature for a few hours. When the meringue has cooled to 30–35°C/86–95°F (at which point it is ready to use), add the butter, whisking vigorously until smooth. If you wish, flavour the buttercream with a little pistachio paste, cocoa powder, vanilla extract or coffee essence.

Use this light buttercream as a filling for sponge cakes (see page 255) or choux buns (see page 174).

French meringues

Makes 350g (12oz)
(serves 6–8)

4 medium egg whites

125g (scant ²/3 cup) caster
(superfine) sugar

125g (1 cup) icing (confectioners')
sugar, sifted

for the flavourings (optional)

coffee essence

raspberry or lemon essence

cocoa powder

My favourite flavourings for these meringues are coffee,
lemon and vanilla. I sometimes dip the base of the coffee
meringues in melted chocolate ... naughty but nice.

In a bowl, beat the egg whites with a balloon whisk until they form
soft peaks. Still whisking continuously, shower in the caster sugar,
a little at a time, and continue to whisk for about 10 minutes, until
the mixture is smooth and shiny, and holds firm points on the whisk
when you lift it out of the mixture. Shower in the icing sugar and
fold it in with a spatula. (Alternatively, you can use an electric mixer.)

The meringue is now ready to make plain meringues. For flavoured
meringues, divide between 2 or 3 bowls and flavour as you wish:
stir in a few drops of coffee essence, or a few drops of raspberry or
lemon essence, or ½–1 tsp cocoa powder.

Preheat the oven to 110°C/225°F/Gas ¼. Using a tablespoon, shape
the meringue into large quenelles and place them on a baking
sheet lined with baking parchment, or pipe them using a plain or
fluted nozzle if you prefer. Cook in the oven for 1¼ hours for small
meringues, or allow an extra 5–10 minutes for larger ones.

When the meringues are ready, switch off the oven and leave them
to cool inside for several hours. I like to serve these meringues as
petits fours, or with ice cream. They keep well for several days in
an airtight container stored in a dry place.

*To make meringue nests, spoon or
pipe the meringue into ovals, about
8 x 4cm (3¼–1½in), and make a
hollow in the middle with the back
of a spoon dipped in water. Bake as
above, allowing 1½ hours.*

Pavlova with berries, mango & passion fruit

SERVES 8

1 quantity French meringue (see page 244)

1 mango

100g (3½oz) strawberries or wild strawberries

100g (3½oz) raspberries

100g (3½oz) redcurrants

100g (3½oz) blackberries

100g (3½oz) blueberries

400ml (1¾ cups) double (heavy) cream

1 tbsp rosewater (optional)

4 passion fruit, halved

caster (superfine) or icing (confectioners') sugar, to dust

This is undoubtedly one of the finest desserts in the world. My Australian wife, Robyn, and Bette, her mother, make the best pavlovas I have ever tasted. The fruits you use must be ripe, very sweet and full of flavour.

Preheat the oven to 150°C/300°F/Gas 2. Line a baking sheet with baking parchment and spread the meringue into a rough disc, 22 cm (8½in) in diameter, 5 cm (2in) high. Cook in the oven for 30 minutes, then lower the setting to 120°C/250°F/Gas ½ and cook for another 45 minutes.

Switch off the oven and leave the pavlova inside to cool for at least 6–8 hours, or preferably overnight. It should then be half-cooked in the middle, crisp on the outside, and the edges should be slightly cracked.

Peel and thinly slice the mango off the stone. Rinse the berries in cold water if necessary, hull or de-stalk them, and place on kitchen paper to dry.

Carefully peel off the parchment and place the pavlova on a flat serving plate. Whip the cream with the rosewater to a very light ribbon consistency, then spoon on top of the pavlova. Scatter the fruits over the surface, and then spoon the passion fruit pulp and seeds over the top. Dust with sugar and serve at once.

Salzburger nockerl

SERVES 4

20g (1½ tbsp) butter, to grease

6 egg yolks

75g (heaped ½ cup) icing (confectioners') sugar, plus extra to dust

2 vanilla pods, split

4 medium egg whites

100g (½ cup) caster (superfine) sugar

To serve

400g (14oz) wild strawberries

I sometimes top warm vanilla-flavoured apple compote with this meringue mixture and bake it briefly as above ... give it a try.

A cross between a meringue and a soufflé, this has a melting texture and a vanilla aroma – perfect with strawberries and ice cream.

Preheat the oven to 180°C/350°F/Gas 4 and butter a shallow oval ovenproof dish, measuring about 30 x 20 cm (12 x 8in).

Put the egg yolks and icing sugar into a small bowl. Scrape out the seeds from the vanilla pods and add them to the bowl, then whisk the mixture to a ribbon consistency.

In a separate bowl, whisk the egg whites to a thick foam, then add the caster sugar and whisk until firm and smooth. Delicately fold half the egg whites into the yolk mixture with a skimmer or slotted spoon, then gently fold in the rest.

Immediately, spoon the meringue mixture into the buttered dish, heaping it into 2 or 3 little mounds, then smooth it with a palette knife. Bake at once in the oven for 3–4 minutes, just long enough to half-cook the meringue and to colour it lightly.

As soon as the meringue comes out of the oven, dust with icing sugar and arrange the strawberries around the edge. Serve immediately.

Floating islands

Serve this with a bowl of fresh berries, if they are in season.

1 litre (4 cups) milk

190g (scant 1 cup) caster (superfine) sugar

6 medium egg whites

groundnut oil, to oil

50g (1¾oz) flaked almonds, lightly toasted

250ml (1 cup) crème anglaise (see page 202), well chilled (see note)

For the caramel

200g (1 cup) caster (superfine) sugar

Heat the milk and 50g (¼ cup) of the sugar in a wide, shallow pan. As soon as it comes to the boil, lower the heat to maintain a temperature of 70°–80°C/158–176°F.

In a bowl, beat the egg whites to a thick foam, then shower in the remaining 140g (scant ¾ cup) sugar and continue to beat until very firm. Using a large spoon, lift out one-quarter of the meringue and shape into a large quenelle on the spoon with the aid of a palette knife. Dip the spoon into the hot milk; the egg white will slide off into the milk. Rinse the spoon immediately in cold water and repeat to make 4 quenelles or 'islands'.

Poach the meringue islands for 2 minutes, then delicately turn them over in the milk and poach for 2 minutes on the other side until just firm to the touch, but still delicate and light. Use a skimmer to lift out the islands, one at a time, placing them on a tea towel to drain thoroughly. Transfer the islands to a lightly oiled sheet of foil.

To make the caramel, dissolve the sugar in a small saucepan, stirring gently and continuously with a wooden spoon. As soon as it turns to a light golden caramel, spoon it over the islands and immediately scatter on the flaked almonds.

Pour the chilled crème anglaise into a shallow serving bowl and float the caramelised islands on top. Serve at once.

The crème anglaise should be well flavoured with vanilla, so infuse the milk with 2 vanilla pods.

Raspberry macarons

MAKES ABOUT 20

180g (1¼ cups) icing (confectioners') sugar, sifted

100g (1 cup) ground almonds

10g (1½ tbsp) raspberry powder (see note)

3 egg whites

4 drops of red food colouring

40g (3¼ tbsp) caster (superfine) sugar

For the raspberry butter

200g (7oz) fresh raspberries

50g (¼ cup) caster (superfine) sugar

80g (⅓ cup) butter, softened

If you can't find raspberry powder, you can make your own. Spread fresh raspberries out on a baking sheet lined with baking parchment and dry in a warming oven or airing cupboard for 3–4 days. When bone dry, grind the raspberries to a powder in a blender, then rub through a sieve.

These delicate little macarons are very elegant. Serve them simply with coffee, or with ice cream or sorbet.

First make the raspberry butter. Put the raspberries and sugar in a small pan and cook gently for 20 minutes. Whiz in a blender for 1 minute, then pass through a chinois into a bowl. Leave until cold, then gradually whisk into the butter; set aside.

For the macarons, preheat the oven to 160°C/350°F/Gas 2½. Mix together the icing sugar, ground almonds and raspberry powder. Beat the egg whites in a bowl to a thick foam, then add the red colouring and caster sugar, and beat for 1 minute until firm. Gradually shower in the almond mixture, folding it in with a spatula until it is amalgamated. Put the mixture into a piping bag fitted with a plain 1cm (½in) nozzle.

Pipe about 40 rounds on to a baking sheet lined with baking parchment, making them 3–4cm (1¼–1½cm) in diameter and of uniform size. Pipe well apart in staggered rows, so they will cook evenly and won't touch as they spread. Slide the baking sheet on to another one to make a double thickness, and bake the macarons for 7 minutes.

Slide the baking parchment on to a wire rack and leave to cool. When cold, lift the macarons off the paper and sandwich them together in pairs with raspberry butter.

Genoese sponge

MAKES A 20CM (8IN) SPONGE CAKE

20g (1½ tbsp) softened butter, to grease tin

125g (scant 1 cup) plain (all-purpose) flour, plus extra to dust

4 medium eggs, at room temperature

125g (scant ⅔ cup) caster (superfine) sugar

30g (2 tbsp) butter, melted and cooled to tepid

Genoese sponge has an excellent texture and many uses. It also freezes well.

Preheat the oven to 190°C/375°F/Gas 5. Butter and lightly flour a 20cm (8in) cake tin.

Put the eggs and sugar in a bowl and immediately whisk them together. Continue to whisk for about 12 minutes, until the mixture leaves a ribbon trail when you lift the whisk. (You can also do this in an electric mixer.)

Shower in the flour and delicately fold it into the mixture, with a rubber spatula.

Add the melted butter and fold in carefully, without overworking the mixture.

Pour the mixture into the cake tin and bake for 30 minutes, or until it is cooked. To test, lightly press the centre of the sponge with your fingertips; there should be a slight resistance and the sponge should 'sing', emitting a soft 'zzzz'. Invert on to a wire rack, giving the sponge a quarter-turn after 10 minutes to prevent it sticking. Leave to cool for 3–4 hours.

Uses for Genoese sponge

Serve the Genoese plain, cut into thin slices. I love to dunk these in vanilla crème anglaise (see page 202) before eating.

Chocolate Genoese sponge Replace the 125g (scant 1 cup) flour with a mixture of 75g (½ cup) plain (all-purpose) flour and 50g (6 tbsp) cocoa powder, then follow the method for plain Genoese sponge (see page 252).

Layer cake Using a serrated knife, split the Genoese horizontally into two layers. Sandwich together with buttercream (see page 243) and dust the top with caster or icing (confectioners') sugar, or top with another layer of buttercream.

Lamingtons Make 1 quantity of Genoese sponge mixture and cook in a buttered and floured 15cm (6in) square cake tin, which is 4cm (1½in) deep (following the method on page 252). Allow to cool (and, ideally, store in an airtight tin overnight before icing).

For the icing, sift 500g (4 cups) icing (confectioners') sugar with 50g (6 tbsp) cocoa powder into a bowl, then stir in 20g (1½ tbsp) melted butter and 175ml (¾ cup) milk. Stand the bowl over a pan of simmering water and stir until the icing is smooth and a thin coating consistency. Take the bowl off the pan and leave until the icing is cold and slightly thickened. Cut the sponge into 2.5cm (1in) squares. Scatter 350g (4–5 cups) desiccated coconut on a board. Working with 4 or 5 sponge squares at a time, dip into the icing to coat, then roll in the coconut. Leave on a wire rack until set. Serve these little Australian cakes with coffee or tea, or as a dessert with vanilla ice cream (see page 224).

Raspberry roulade

20g (1½ tbsp) softened butter, to grease

flour, to dust

1 quantity Genoese sponge mixture (see page 252)

icing (confectioners') sugar, to dust

For the filling

300ml (1¼ cups) double (heavy) cream

100g (scant ½ cup) crème pâtissière (see page 206)

250g (scant 1 cup) raspberry jelly, or sieved raspberry jam

500g (1lb 2oz) raspberries

Fragrant raspberries make an ideal filling for this roulade, although wild strawberries are equally good when in season. For sheer decadence, serve with a glass of pink Champagne.

Preheat the oven to 180°C/350°F/Gas 4. Lay a 40 x 30cm (16 x 12in) sheet of greaseproof paper on a baking sheet and lightly butter the paper, then dust lightly with flour. Refrigerate or set aside in a cool place.

Using a palette knife, spread the Genoese sponge mixture over the paper in a 1cm (½in) layer. Bake in the oven for 6–8 minutes. Immediately cover the cooked sponge with a tea towel and invert it on the tea towel on to a wire rack. Carefully peel off the paper and set aside to cool for 5 minutes only.

Meanwhile, for the filling, whip the cream to a ribbon consistency, then add the crème pâtissière and mix thoroughly with a whisk.

Fill the roulade as soon as it has just cooled, otherwise it will be difficult to roll. Loosen the raspberry jelly with a whisk and use a palette knife to spread it delicately over the surface of the sponge. Trim all 4 sides with a serrated knife to neaten and remove the crusty edges. Spread the cream mixture over the surface of the sponge, stopping 1cm (½in) short of the edges, then scatter the raspberries evenly over the cream.

Using the tea towel to help you, carefully roll up the sponge from a long side to form a neat roll. Chill for 3–4 hours. Dust the roulade generously with icing sugar to serve.

Chocolate truffle cake with candied kumquats

SERVES 8

475g (1lb 1oz) good-quality dark chocolate (70% cocoa solids), chopped into small pieces

1 chocolate Genoese sponge base, 20cm (8in) in diameter (see page 252)

splash of Cognac or rum

475ml (2 cups) double (heavy) cream

cocoa powder, to dust

For the candied kumquats

16 very ripe kumquats

600g (3 cups) caster (superfine) sugar

This alluring dessert is always popular and it is simple to make. You can prepare both the cake and kumquats a day or two in advance and keep them in the fridge.

First prepare the kumquats. Put them in a small saucepan, cover with cold water and boil for 1 minute, then refresh in cold water. Repeat this twice more; drain. Return to the pan, add 600ml (2½ cups) water and the sugar and slowly bring to the boil. Lower the heat to keep the syrup at 80-90°C/176-194°F and poach the kumquats for 30-45 minutes, until lightly candied. Transfer to a bowl with the syrup and leave until cold.

For the truffle cake, gently melt the chocolate in a bowl over a pan of hot water, then take the bowl off the pan and leave to cool for a few minutes until no less than 25°C/77°C.

Using a serrated knife, cut a 5mm (¼in) thick disc from the chocolate sponge. Place it on a cardboard base and place a pastry ring round the sponge disc. If the sponge seems a little dry, moisten with a little of the kumquat syrup, flavoured with Cognac or rum.

Whip the cream in a large bowl to a ribbon consistency. Fold in half of the melted chocolate with a whisk, then fold in the rest. Whisk very lightly until amalgamated. Pour the mixture into the pastry ring and push it to the edge with a palette knife, taking care not to leave any air holes. Smooth the surface with the palette knife. Put the truffle cake in the fridge for at least 2 hours to firm up.

To serve, warm the pastry ring for a few seconds with a blowtorch, then remove. Dust the top of the cake with cocoa and cut into slices. Serve with the candied kumquats.

Sauces & Dressings

The classic emulsion sauces – hollandaise, mayonnaise and sabayon – rely on the unique properties of eggs. Refined, delicate and airy, hollandaise and sabayon make the most marvellous accompaniments to fish, vegetables and other dishes. They each take only 10 to 15 minutes to prepare and cook, but they will lose their lightness if kept waiting, so serve within 15 minutes of cooking. Mayonnaise is the key to taste heaven. The addition of snipped fresh herbs, chopped hard-boiled eggs, fresh tomato coulis, grated horseradish or a little chlorophyll (see page 270) promotes an explosion of flavours to enhance seafood, smoked fish, hard-boiled eggs, and more. Finally, I use egg yolks to bind and enrich salad dressings, such as my Swiss vinaigrette (see page 280) and Caesar dressing (see page 279), as well as selected sauces (see pages 281–2).

Hollandaise sauce

1 tbsp white wine vinegar

1 tsp white peppercorns, crushed

4 egg yolks

250g (1 cup) butter, clarified
(see page 87) and cooled to tepid

salt

juice of ½ lemon

Hollandaise cannot be kept waiting, so serve it as soon as it is made, or keep it covered for a short time in a warm place if you must.

In a saucepan, mix the wine vinegar with 4 tbsp cold water and the pepper. Reduce by one-third and leave to cool completely.

Add the egg yolks to the cold reduction and mix with a whisk. Put the saucepan on a heat diffuser over a very low heat and continue whisking, making sure that the whisk comes into contact with the bottom of the pan.

Gradually increase the heat so that the sauce emulsifies progressively, becoming very smooth and creamy after 8–10 minutes. Do not allow the temperature of the sauce to rise above 65°C/150°F.

Off the heat and still whisking, pour in the tepid clarified butter in a steady stream. Season the sauce with salt. At the last moment, stir in the lemon juice. Pass the sauce through a muslin-lined chinois to eliminate the crushed peppercorns if required, then serve immediately.

VARIATION To make a noisette sauce, add 50g (3½ tbsp) foaming browned butter to the finished hollandaise. This sauce is even more delicate than a hollandaise, and it's particularly good with fish.

Mustard hollandaise

SERVES 6

75ml (5 tbsp) double (heavy) cream

30g (2 tbsp) strong Dijon mustard

1 quantity freshly made hollandaise sauce (see page 262)

salt and freshly ground pepper

This mildly piquant sauce enhances the flavour of salmon without overpowering it. Try it with grilled salmon steaks and samphire (as shown). It's also delicious with steamed courgettes.

Whip the cream in a bowl to a ribbon consistency, then mix in the mustard until evenly blended.

Whisk the mustard cream little by little into the hollandaise. Season with salt and pepper to taste and serve immediately.

If preferred, use 1 tbsp English mustard powder dissolved in a few drops of warm water in place of the Dijon mustard.

Mayonnaise

Makes about 300ml (1¼ cups)

2 egg yolks, at room temperature

1 tbsp strong Dijon mustard

salt and freshly ground pepper

250ml (1 cup) groundnut oil,
at room temperature

2 tbsp white wine vinegar or
lemon juice

Mayonnaise has many uses, but it's especially good with fish and seafood. It can be kept for several hours in a cold place, covered with cling film.

Stand a mixing bowl on a tea towel on the work surface. Put the egg yolks, mustard and a little salt and pepper into the bowl and mix with a balloon whisk.

Slowly add the oil in a thin trickle to begin with, whisking continuously.

As the mayonnaise begins to thicken, add the oil in a steady stream, still whisking all the time.

When the oil is completely incorporated, whisk more rapidly for 30 seconds, until the mayonnaise is thick and glossy. Add the vinegar or lemon juice, taste, and adjust the seasoning as necessary.

Mayonnaise variations

Creamy mayonnaise Stir in 2 tbsp double (heavy) cream after adding the vinegar or lemon juice.

Light mayonnaise For a less rich mayonnaise, simply substitute egg whites for the egg yolks.

Bagnarotte sauce Flavour one quantity of mayonnaise (see page 266) with 3 tbsp tomato ketchup, ½ tsp Worcestershire sauce, 1 tbsp Cognac (optional), 2 tbsp double (heavy) cream, 6 drops of Tabasco and the juice of ½ lemon. Whisk well to combine and season with salt and pepper to taste. Refrigerate until ready to use. This refreshing sauce is delicious with fresh crab, ripe tomatoes and cucumber, and with poached eggs (see page 42) or hard-boiled eggs (see page 18).

Low-fat mayonnaise In a mixing bowl, whisk 150 g (²/₃ cup) fromage blanc or fromage frais (0% fat) with 1 egg yolk, 1 tsp strong Dijon mustard and 1 tbsp white wine vinegar or lemon juice until completely smooth. Season with salt and pepper to taste. If you wish, stir in a little snipped fresh mint, chives or tarragon, or some chervil leaves, just before serving.

Green mayonnaise

SERVES 6

1 quantity mayonnaise (see page 266)

salt and freshly ground pepper

For the chlorophyll

200g (7oz) spinach, stalks removed

10g (⅓oz) chervil, stalks removed

20g (⅔oz) flat leaf parsley, stalks removed

10g (⅓oz) tarragon, stalks removed

10g (⅓oz) chives

10g (⅓oz) shallot, thinly sliced

A simple hard-boiled egg with this amazing sauce is a treat. I also like to serve it alongside a medley of smoked fish and shellfish (eel, trout, mackerel, oysters, mussels, etc), on toasted baguette slices – as tapas.

To make the chlorophyll, wash and dry the spinach and herb leaves, then put into a blender or electric herb chopper. Add the shallot and 350 ml (1½ cups) water and whiz for 1 minute at low speed, then for another 4 minutes at medium speed.

Loosely drape a piece of muslin over a saucepan and secure it with an elastic band. Pour the herb purée into the muslin and let it drip through slowly. After 10 minutes, gather up the edges of the muslin and squeeze to extract as much liquid as possible. Discard the herb residue and rinse the muslin in cold water.

Gently heat the green liquid in the pan, stirring delicately with a wooden spoon. As soon as the liquid starts to tremble, take the pan off the heat. Loosely drape the muslin over a bowl and secure with an elastic band. Delicately ladle the green liquid on to the muslin and leave to drain through for about 20 minutes. Use a spatula to scrape off the soft green chlorophyll from the surface of the muslin and put it into a ramekin. (It will keep for several days in the fridge covered with a little groundnut oil.)

To make the green mayonnaise, whisk a spoonful or two of the chlorophyll into the mayonnaise, to taste. Check the seasoning, then serve.

Classic sabayon

SERVES 4

100ml (scant ½ cup) Sauternes or other sweet white wine

3 egg yolks

40g (2½ tbsp) caster (superfine) sugar

You will need a cooking thermometer to check the temperature of the sabayon.

Two-thirds fill a saucepan (large enough to hold a round-bottomed bowl) with warm water, and heat gently. Pour the Sauternes into the bowl, then add the egg yolks, whisking as you go. Carry on whisking as you shower in the sugar.

Continue whisking the mixture over the heat so that it gradually thickens, making sure that the temperature of the water in the pan increases steadily but moderately.

After 8–10 minutes, the mixture should have reached a light ribbon consistency. It is essential to keep whisking all the time. When the temperature reaches 55°C/131°F, the sabayon is cooked.

Turn off the heat and continue whisking until the sabayon has a very thick ribbon consistency and a fluffy, rich and shiny texture. Remove the bowl from the pan. Serve the sabayon immediately, in glasses.

VARIATION Replace the Sauternes with Banyuls or Marsala, or with an eau-de-vie, such as raspberry or pear. For an eau-de-vie sabayon, use 75ml (5 tbsp) eau-de-vie and 50ml (3½ tbsp) water, and increase the sugar by 50%.

Chocolate sabayon

150g (¾ cup) caster (superfine) sugar

4 egg yolks

50g (6 tbsp) cocoa powder

finely grated zest of 1 orange

Try serving this sabayon topped with little choux buns sprinkled with a few flaked almonds ... delicious.

Put the sugar in a small saucepan with 150ml (scant ⅔ cup) water and dissolve over a low heat, then bring to the boil and immediately turn off the heat. Leave the sugar syrup to cool completely.

Two-thirds fill a saucepan (large enough to hold a round-bottomed bowl) with warm water, and heat gently. Pour the sugar syrup into the bowl, then whisk in the egg yolks.

Continue whisking the mixture over the heat (see page 272), for about 8–10 minutes until the sabayon is a light ribbon consistency. When the sabayon reaches 65°C/149°F, it is ready. Turn off the heat and continue whisking until the sabayon has a very thick ribbon consistency and a fluffy, rich and shiny texture.

Remove the bowl from the saucepan, then sprinkle in the cocoa powder, a little at a time, whisking delicately until it has dissolved. Stir in the grated orange zest without overworking the sabayon. Spoon the sabayon into glasses and serve immediately.

Spinach & watercress sabayon

SERVES 4

100g (3½oz) baby spinach leaves

50g (1¾oz) watercress leaves

salt and freshly ground pepper

2 egg yolks

40g (3 tbsp) butter, diced

If preferred, use 1 tbsp English mustard powder dissolved in a few drops of warm water in place of the Dijon mustard.

I use this fresh-tasting sabayon to coat my mollet egg & courgette tarts, (see right, recipe page 27). It's also good with cauliflower or broccoli, or tossed with spaghetti and sprinkled with Parmesan.

Wash the spinach and watercress leaves, then drain well. Bring 100ml (scant ½ cup) lightly salted water to the boil in a saucepan. Immediately drop in the spinach and watercress leaves, cook for 1 minute, then tip the mixture into a blender and whiz for 1 minute. Pass the purée through a chinois into a small bowl, then set over ice to cool the mixture quickly.

Two-thirds fill a saucepan (large enough to hold a round-bottomed bowl) with warm water, and heat gently. Pour the spinach and watercress purée into the bowl and set over the pan. Add the egg yolks, whisking as you go.

Whisk the mixture constantly for 8–10 minutes (see page 272), until it has a light ribbon consistency. When the sabayon reaches 70°C/158°F, it is ready.

Remove the bowl from the saucepan, then gradually whisk in the diced butter. The sabayon should have a rich, shiny texture. Season with salt and pepper to taste and serve immediately.

Caesar dressing

SERVES 6

1 egg yolk

⅛ tsp Dijon mustard

1 tbsp lemon juice

⅛ garlic clove, crushed

1 tsp bottled anchovy essence

75 ml (5 tbsp) groundnut oil

30 g (1 oz) Parmesan, freshly grated

freshly ground pepper

This dressing is particularly good with robust salad leaves, such as Cos. It is the dressing used in my Caesar salad with poached eggs (see left, recipe page 53).

Put the egg yolk, mustard, lemon juice and crushed garlic in a bowl, and blend with a small whisk until very smooth.

Add the anchovy essence, then slowly whisk in the groundnut oil until amalgamated. Add the grated Parmesan, and finally whisk in 2 tbsp water to give a slightly looser consistency. Season the dressing with pepper to taste.

Swiss vinaigrette

SERVES 6

20g (²/₃oz) shallot, finely chopped

½ garlic clove, crushed and chopped

pinch of sugar

1 egg yolk

1 tsp Maggi liquid seasoning (available in supermarkets)

2 tbsp double (heavy) cream

6 tbsp groundnut oil

2 tbsp white wine vinegar

salt and freshly ground pepper

I love the flavour of this creamy vinaigrette, which goes perfectly with my mollet eggs on crabmeat & celeriac julienne (see page 31) and mollet bantam eggs with rocket & Parmesan shavings (see page 26). It is also brilliant with a Cos lettuce or escarole salad.

Put all the ingredients, except the oil, wine vinegar and salt and pepper, in a bowl. Mix thoroughly with a whisk for a minute or two, then pour in the groundnut oil in a thin steady stream, whisking as you go. Finally, whisk in the wine vinegar and season with salt and pepper to taste.

Sauce écossaise

SERVES 4–6

60g (2oz) carrot, finely diced

50g (1¾oz) celery, finely diced

60g (2oz) green beans, finely diced

50g (1¾oz) onion, finely diced

50g (3½ tbsp) butter

50ml (3½ tbsp) double (heavy) cream

1 egg yolk

juice of 1 lemon

salt and freshly ground pepper

For the béchamel

30g (2 tbsp) butter

30g (3½ tbsp) plain (all-purpose) flour

500ml (2 cups) milk

This sauce is the perfect accompaniment for my poached eggs on potatoes with smoked haddock (see page 49).

First make a béchamel. Melt the butter in a small, heavy-based saucepan over a low heat, then add the flour, stir with a whisk, and cook gently for 2–3 minutes to make a white roux. Pour the cold milk on to the roux, as you whisk, and bring to the boil over a medium heat, whisking continuously. When the sauce comes to the boil, lower the heat and simmer gently for about 7 minutes, stirring at regular intervals.

Meanwhile, blanch the vegetables in boiling water for 1 minute. Refresh in cold water, drain and pat dry. Melt the butter in a small saucepan, add the blanched vegetables and sweat gently for 2–3 minutes.

Add the vegetables to the béchamel and let the sauce bubble for 2–3 minutes. Mix the cream and egg yolk together, then stir into the sauce. As soon it comes back to the boil, stir in the lemon juice and remove from the heat. Season the sauce with salt and pepper to taste. It is now ready to serve.

For an egg gratin, arrange sliced hard-boiled eggs in a well-buttered ovenproof dish, coat thickly with sauce écossaise and heat in the oven at 180°C/350°F/Gas 4 for 5 minutes.

Mornay sauce

30g (2 tbsp) butter

30g (3½ tbsp) plain (all-purpose) flour

500ml (2 cups) milk

pinch of freshly grated nutmeg

salt and freshly ground white pepper

3 egg yolks

50ml (3½ tbsp) double cream

100g (3½oz) Gruyère, Emmenthal or Cheddar, finely grated

Coat broccoli with this sauce and top with cheese (see right) for a tasty vegetable dish. I also use it for my poached eggs florentine (see page 46), to make macaroni cheese, and in my chicken & mushroom crêpes (see page 161).

First make a béchamel. Melt the butter in a small, heavy-based saucepan over a low heat, then add the flour, stir with a whisk, and cook gently for 2–3 minutes to make a white roux. Pour the cold milk on to the roux, as you whisk, and bring to the boil over a medium heat, whisking continuously. When the sauce comes to the boil, lower the heat and simmer gently for about 10 minutes, stirring frequently. Season to taste with nutmeg, salt and white pepper.

Mix the egg yolks and cream together in a bowl, then pour the mixture into the béchamel, whisking as you do so. Let the sauce bubble for about 1 minute, whisking continuously, then take the pan off the heat and shower in the grated cheese. Stir until melted, then taste and adjust the seasoning if necessary.

Index